HOW TO WATCH BASEBALL

HOW TO WATCH BASEBALL

Steve Fiffer

Facts On File Publications
New York, New York ● Oxford, England

Library of Congress Cataloguing-in-Publication Data
Fiffer, Steve.
　How to watch baseball.
　Includes index.
　1. Baseball. I. Title.
GV867.F43 1987　　796.357'2　　　86-24064
ISBN 0-8160-1354-3　hc
ISBN 0-8160-2001-9　pb

Composition by Facts On File/Maxwell Photographics
Printed in the United States of America

10 9 8 7 6 5 4 3 2

To Kate and Nora . . . Watching you is terrific.

ACKNOWLEDGMENTS

The author wishes to thank all the major league ballclubs, players, managers, and coaches who helped make researching this book such an enjoyable experience. Carlton Fisk, Ken "Hawk" Harrelson, Dick Howser, Walt Hriniak, and Dave Nelson were particularly invaluable. Special thanks to Paul Jensen of the Chicago White Sox and Sharon Pannozzo of the Chicago Cubs for allowing me to roam their ballparks. Thanks also to Gaylord Broadcasting Company, *Inside Sports* (particularly Vince Aversano), Jane Jordan Browne, Gerry Helferich, and Sharon Fiffer.

Chapters 5 and 6 have appeared in slightly different form in *Inside Sports* magazine.

Baseball, like sex and religion, is a complicated game to play, but not hard to understand.
—George V. Higgins, author and Boston Red Sox fan

CONTENTS

Preface xi

1. Before the Game: Details, Details, Details 1
2. Pitching: The Heart of the Game 19
3. Hitting: No Place to Hide 51
4. Defense: The Ballet No One Watches 71
5. Base Stealing: The Guessing Game 93
6. The Manager: Keeping the Team in the Game 111
7. On-Field Communication: Cries and Whispers 137
8. What the Box Score Doesn't Reveal: Watching
     with the Experts 155
9. Watching the Players: The Ultimate Lesson 179

Index 195

PREFACE

In the 1950s and 1960s, there were two mortal sins of which a Chicagoan could be guilty: being a Republican and being a New York Yankees fan. If I had been old enough, I would have voted the straight Democratic ticket as my parents did at each election. No trouble there. But, father, forgive me, I was a Yankees fanatic.

As the local White Sox were perennial runners-up to the Stengel dynasty, my friends showered me with charges of desertion. I barely heard them. I had the radio to my ear so I could listen to the Bombers win another World Series.

Sometimes I think, Freud and Spock be damned, it was the Yankees that shaped my growth. Doesn't it make sense that I never learned to accept losing because the Yankees of my childhood so rarely lost? At the very least, the team dictated certain preferences. My favorite color was "pinstripe." My favorite number was 7 (after my hero Mickey Mantle, of course). I don't remember what my favorite city after New York was, but most likely it was Commerce, Oklahoma, the Mick's hometown.

I did all the things a fan 800 miles away from his idols could do. I saw the Yankees every time they came to town and sent away for their yearbook; I scoured the public library for books about the team, living in constant fear that some diehard Sox fan would attempt to have such material banned as heretical. Two things consumed me: Mantle and The Tradition. I knew everything there was to know about Mickey and was surely Chicago's leading authority on the Yankees' history, which seemed embodied in The House That Ruth Built, Yankee Stadium.

As rewarding as it was to have my heroes in the World Series each fall, I was frustrated. More than anything else I wanted Mickey Mantle's autograph. And more than anything except getting the autograph, I wanted to see a game in Yankee Stadium. In the spring of 1959, just a few months short of my ninth birthday, I set out to reach those goals.

Getting Mantle's signature was my first priority. I thought long and hard about how to achieve this. I had already tried waiting outside Comiskey Park when the Yanks were in Chicago. No luck. A friend suggested that Mickey probably snuck out in a disguise, as boxer Floyd Patterson was wont to do, but I knew I would have recognized him no matter what the costume. I reasoned that there must be a secret passage out of the ball park reserved for the Williamses and Mantles so they wouldn't get crushed.

Another friend said I should wait at the hotel where the Yankees stayed. But my father, tolerant as he was with my fixation, refused to spend a day in some lobby on the off-chance that the Commerce Comet would appear. Did he know then what Jim Bouton would reveal years later: that the chances of finding Mickey in his hotel were about the same as keeping him off the bases?

I finally decided to write him. I was composing the letter when the brainstorm struck. Why not invite him for dinner? It must be hard on players when they travel, I reasoned. They miss all that great home cooking that gives them the strength to go out and hit home runs. It must be lonely, too, away from the family. We were a terrific family, and my mom was a terrific cook, I wrote Mickey. He could come anytime, and my mother would prepare whatever he wanted. What did he want? Mom made excellent liver, which was supposed to be quite good for you.

I sent the letter off (as well as letters to every other Yankee—autograph request only, no dinner invitation), convinced our household would soon be hosting the most famous visitor our neighborhood had ever seen, that pretty soon I'd be sitting across the table from my hero, passing the ketchup and hearing what it was like to be a Yankee.

While waiting for Mickey to respond with his choice of evening and menu, I attempted to orchestrate my second wish—seeing a game at Yankee Stadium. Our family always took a vacation at the end of the summer. In late April I suggested that it might be nice to spend that time out East, say in the Bronx. The "out East" part of my proposal was adopted, with the caveat that the date of our visit to New York would be contingent on when my father could get away from his office; the Yankees might be out of town. I didn't argue. There was no team at all in the Wisconsin Dells, our second vacation choice. Besides, I believed that if there were any justice in the world, a fan as loyal as I was would be rewarded.

The Yankees made their first of three trips to Chicago early in the season. Mickey had not responded to my invitation, a state of affairs that I chose to blame on the U.S. Postal Service . . . or his teammates. The Yankees were off to a slow start; Mantle probably wanted to come to the house when things were looking up.

Things *were* looking up when they returned several weeks later. And I had begun to hear from some of the Yankees. Bob Turley, Duke Maas. But not Mantle. Did pitchers have more time to write? I began to think it was a mistake to mention that my mom's specialty was liver.

It was soon time for our vacation. My dad had some business to transact in Boston, so we still didn't know if we'd be in New York when the Yankees were there. I wasn't sure if I could stand the double disappointment of being stood up by

Mantle and missing Yankee Stadium. Make that triple disappointment. Listening to the games as we drove East (my
Yankees yearbook had a complete list of stations carrying the
team games), it became clear that the Yanks were going to lose
their first pennant since 1954 and that the hated White Sox
might succeed them.

Still, the Yankees dominated my consciousness. On the
road, my brother and I played a game in which we tried to
guess how much everything cost—food, gas, lodging. My
parents found this gauche and ordered us to stop. But we
developed our own code, using Yankees' uniform numbers.
Thus, if we thought the gas would be $4.25 (remember this
was 1959), we said, "Gehrig-Crosetti-DiMaggio." If the food
was, "Lopez-Ruth-Berra," my father had shelled out $11.38.

The hotel in New York must have cost at least Casey Stengel
dollars a night. We had adjoining rooms on an upper floor
with a view of Central Park. If I had been able to open a
window, I might have jumped: The Yankees were out of
town. I brooded so much the first day that if my parents had
been able to open a window, they might have *thrown* me out.

On our second morning in the city, my mother and I
returned from a walk to find my father holding his camera
and looking very proud of himself. "I called Yankee
Stadium," he said. "I told them I had the greatest Yankees fan
outside of New York. They said we could come down and see
the ball park."

The pictures take up several pages of the family album, but
27 years later I don't need them to refresh my memory. I
remember walking onto the field and running out to center,
where my hero patrolled. I remember reading the plaques in
the outfield, sitting in the same dugout that Ruth, DiMaggio,
and now Mantle had sat in. I remember posing with the
batboy (who happened to be there) and wishing like anything
I could have his job. And most of all, I remember playing a
make-believe game of baseball with my brother.

When we got back to Chicago, there was a letter. I still have
it. Framed, it now shares a wall with a note from John F.

Kennedy. "This will acknowledge receipt of your recent communication," the message on Yankees' letterhead read. "It is a pleasure to receive such encouraging mail. Thank you for your interest in the Yankees which you have demonstrated by taking the time to write. Sincerely yours . . ."

It was signed "Mickey Mantle."

There was no mention of my dinner invitation, but I didn't care. I had my autograph, and I had the memories of that day in the Bronx. After all, how many people can say they've played in Yankee Stadium?

Times change—now I pull for the White Sox instead of the Yankees—but my love for baseball has remained constant. One reason baseball is so enduring is because it is both a simple and a complex game. On its simplest level, it can be understood by even the newest fan. The pitcher pitches; the hitter hits; the runner runs; the fielder fields. On this level the game is seen as a battle between two teams, each of which is trying to score more runs, and as a forum for the exhibition of remarkable individual skills.

But there is more than meets the *untrained* eye. A wondrous subtext. Beneath the simple battle there are numerous skirmishes taking place on and off the field, before, during, and after the nine-inning contest. Because of the game's delightful pace—there is time between each pitch, time between each play—the baseball fan has a unique opportunity to savor this subtext. To second-guess the events of the moment past. To boldly predict the events of the future. To argue over a particular play or strategy.

A symphony can be enjoyed by someone who knows very little about its composer, its content, its subtleties. But it can be enjoyed even more by the person who knows how to listen. A painting is better enjoyed by the person who knows how to look.

Baseball, too, is an art form, and if you know *how to watch*, you can greatly expand your appreciation of the game. That is the simple premise of this book: all of us can better enjoy the sport if we know certain things to look for on the field—the positioning of fielders, base runners "reading" pitchers' pick-off moves. We can also enjoy more if we know about the things going on that we can't actually see—what catchers and umpires talk about during a game, the players' conversation in the dugout.

This book is written for those of you who are interested in the cat-and-mouse game going on between a Wade Boggs at the plate and a Ted Higuera on the mound; those of you who are willing to take your eye off the pitcher for a moment and watch the tricks being played by an outstanding shortstop like Ozzie Smith; those of you who wonder how a manager like Tony LaRussa juggles all the variables he encounters in the course of a game.

As a longtime fan who has written on the sport for the past several years, I consider myself a relatively sophisticated watcher. But as I spent more and more time talking to baseball people—the players, the managers, the coaches—I began to see things I'd never seen before. For example, only recently did I learn that certain hitters will feign the inability to hit a particular kind of pitch early in a game, with the hope that they will see that pitch (which they can in fact hit quite well) later on, when the contest is on the line. Or that you can tell if a pitcher is on his game by watching, of all things, his belt.

I once asked George Brett, the Kansas City Royals' third baseman nonpareil, how he thought a fan should watch baseball. In addition to being one of the all-time great hitters, Brett is an astute and witty observer of the game. "With a hot dog and a beer," he deadpanned.

He's right, of course. There's no need to make things overly complicated. It's not essential that I move my eye away from the batter and watch a base stealer like Vince Coleman change the tempo of the game. It's not crucial that I be able to anticipate the next pitch or stratagem by focusing on the in-terplay between teammates Lou Whitaker at second base and

Alan Trammell at shortstop. But, forgive me, George, I suspect there are countless fans who are hungry to know more about baseball and thirsty for their friends, spouses, and children to know more, too.

My oldest daughter is now the same age I was when I wrote to Mickey Mantle. She collects stickers instead of baseball cards and hopes the Fabulous Chicken will be at the ball park when we go, but she is beginning to ask more questions about what's going on in the field. My wife, who has recently been bitten by the baseball bug, finds it fascinating that pitchers don't always try to throw strikes. My brother, a baseball zealot, is amazed when I tell him that some first-base coaches use stopwatches during the game to time opposing pitchers' deliveries. That information in hand, they then decide whether or not their men should try to steal bases. It is for this spectrum of spectators that I write.

This book is not your normal "how-to" manual. Baseball is not like plumbing or avoiding probate; it remains a game, exciting and, most important, ever—changing and uncertain. It should not be (and perhaps it cannot be) reduced to a dry, analytical presentation. By focusing on specific players and teams that know how to play the game and by presenting their knowledge in what I hope is literate fashion, I have tried to write the kind of book that a casual fan will give as a gift to a sophisticated fan, and then, having devoured it, the sophisticated fan will turn around and give it back to the novice, saying, "See, this is why I love the game."

Why do I love the game? Consider for a moment the warning track, that band of sandy ground extending inward from the outfield wall. "Be careful," it cautions the fielder as he backpedals for the long fly ball or races for the deep line drive. "Feel me underfoot and know that you are off the grass now, on a collision course with a ton of bricks." Would that life outside the ball park were so kind as to warn us every time disaster looms.

1

BEFORE THE GAME: DETAILS, DETAILS, DETAILS

By morning the thunderstorm that had canceled the previous day's ball game had moved well to the east and Wrigley Field was bathed in sunlight. At 7 A.M., Groundskeeper Frank Capparelli and his five-man crew removed the tarpaulin under which the field had slept and began their daily ministrations. Normally, the crew smooths and waters the dirt around home plate, the mound, and the infield and cuts the grass (if necessary) immediately after a game has ended. But the rain put a damper on that routine, and work normally done at dusk must be done at dawn today. The men moved briskly, for although the Chicago Cubs–New York Mets game was not to begin for over seven hours, players and coaches from both teams would soon be arriving at the park.

Indeed, at about 9:15, a taxi pulled up to the corner of Clark and Addison. A man climbed out and entered the park through a special gate. Once inside, he walked past the dormant concession booths under the stands, opened an un-marked door on the first-base side of the field, climbed a flight of stairs, opened another door, and settled into the visitors' clubhouse. Soon Vern Hoscheit was in his uniform, number 51.

Hoscheit, a baseball lifer, has been coming early to ball parks since he broke into the minor leagues as a catcher in 1941. He is 64 now and his jersey has lost the battle with age to contain his friendly stomach. When he talks he sounds a great deal like the old character actor Edgar Buchanan. Although he never made it to the big leagues as a player, he has done just about everything else there is to do in baseball, serving as a minor-league manager and general manager, the president of the old Three-I League, a scout, and even as a spring training chauffeur for the late Casey Stengel. He was a coach on the Oakland Athletics teams that won three world championships in a row from 1972 to 1974 and has been with the Mets since 1983. Lest we neglect his off-the-field calling, it should be noted that he is also the owner of the Shortstop Liquor Store in his hometown of Plainview, Nebraska. Hoscheit's official title is bullpen coach, but he calls himself "details coach," which is, indeed, a more accurate description. For without the detail work that Hoscheit accomplishes during the five hours between the time he arrives at the park and the time the first pitch is thrown, the talented Mets might be in a muddle.

Although you will never see a less likely looking analyst of computer printouts, that is exactly what Hoscheit does first thing each morning for manager Davey Johnson (Johnson's fascination with computers is understandable; he holds a degree in mathematics). "Every day I get information that tells me what our hitters are supposed to be able to do against the opposing pitchers and what the opposing hitters are supposed to do against our pitchers," says Hoscheit. "Today we're facing Mr. [Dennis] Eckersley, so I'll take all the information about how well our guys have hit him and have it on the manager's desk before he gets to the ball park." Johnson usually determines his lineup the night before a game, but the details Hoscheit provides are essential in determining whom to pinch-hit against particular opposing pitchers and which Mets' relief pitchers to bring in to face particular opposing hitters.

When he finally finishes his work with the printouts, Hoscheit moves to a second set of details—the scouting reports. The Mets, like most major-league organizations, employ advance scouts to follow an opponent during the days just prior to their meeting. Thus, a New York scout was in Philadelphia earlier in the week watching the Cubs play the Phillies. His report chronicles every pitch thrown by every Chicago pitcher and the result, and every pitch thrown to every Cubs batter and the result. If a ball is hit into play, the scout even charts where on the field the ball went. The information is particularly helpful in determining how to position the Mets' fielders.

Hoscheit absorbs the material, then puts it out for the players on a table in the middle of the locker room. "See this?" he says pointing to a chart. "This shows where [Cubs' left fielder] Gary Matthews hits the fastball, where he hits the breaking ball. Now our second baseman Wally Backman can look at it before the game and know how to position himself. Or here, you can see that [Cubs' right fielder] Keith Moreland is a better two-strike hitter and that he's gonna hit to the right side. We'll play him accordingly."

The reports even list the fastest and slowest delivery times of the opposing pitchers. Hoscheit culls that information and records it on the lineup card to be posted at game time in the Mets' dugout. According to the scout, starting pitcher Eckersley's fastest delivery—from the time the ball was released until it hit the catcher's glove—was 1.36 seconds; his slowest delivery was 1.48. Relief pitcher George Frazier's range was 1.27 to 1.45. How are these utilized? "Davey can look at them during the game and determine if we can steal off a particular pitcher," explains Hoscheit, who is no longer alone in the clubhouse.

Trainer Steve Garland, assistant trainer Bob Sikes, and rookie infielder-outfielder Kevin Mitchell have arrived. Just as a racehorse can't compete without the help of a trainer, neither can most ball players, particularly those suffering the injuries or aches and pains inevitable during a 162-game season. "Most fans don't realize it, but at any given time at least one and probably three or four of the 24 men on the roster are really hurting," says Garland. "We don't publicize it because we don't want other teams to take advantage of those injuries." Garland recalls a trip to Cincinnati some years ago: "All the papers reported that Pete Rose was taking injections in a sore arm. Reading that, all our guys decided to take an extra base on him whenever they had the chance."

Mitchell, a stocky 24-year-old who looks like he should be carrying a football rather than playing left field, heads today's list of walking wounded. He woke up yesterday with muscle spasms in his back, and they are bothering him again this morning. He does not know what is causing them, but he does know the only way he'll be able to take the field is if Garland and Sikes can loosen him up. Treatment takes almost an hour: 10 minutes in the whirlpool, moist heating packs on the back for 15 minutes, 10 minutes of ultrasound, 12 minutes of a combination of ultrasound and galvanic stimulation, and, finally, massage and stretching. The end result? "Kevin's so muscular that it's hard to get him better," sighs Garland. "You really just try to get him playable and hope that nothing bad happens."

By the time Mitchell is out of the training room, manager Johnson and the rest of the Mets' coaches have arrived, as have some of the players. It is not yet 11:00. The game does not begin until 2:20, and the Mets cannot take the field for batting practice until the Cubs vacate it at 12:50, but there is work to be done. Ordinarily, pitching coach Mel Stottlemyre would begin his day by charting the performance of the pitchers who saw action yesterday, but because the game was rained out his first stop is Johnson's office. He gives Johnson a report on what he'd like to do with the pitchers today. "I tell Dave who I feel will be most available in relief, who's had the most rest, who's best to bring in after the starter, and then we discuss whether we want to give any extra work to a pitcher who hasn't thrown for awhile," he says. Many fans don't realize that, particularly when it comes to pitching, a manager must not only deal with the game at hand, but the upcoming games as well. Like a chess player, he is always several moves ahead in planning his rotation and determining how to utilize his relief pitchers. Yesterday's starter Bob Ojeda has been temporarily bumped from the rotation because of the rainout and manager and coach decide he should throw before today's game.

Stottlemyre returns to his locker and takes a seat next to third-base coach Bud Harrelson and first-base coach Bill Robinson. Harrelson, who played shortstop for the Mets from 1965 to 1977, is reading the *Chicago Tribune* sports section. Like most managers, coaches, and ball players, he reads the box scores of all games played the previous day. "When we're at home at the breakfast table, my wife will complain that she's talking to the top of my head," says Harrelson, laughing. "I've always got my nose buried in the paper." Is there useful information to be gained from the box scores? "Sure," says the coach. "You can tell who's hot, who's not, who drove in runs. I like to see who got walked, maybe learn if a team pitched around a hitter figuring they'd rather have some other hitter beat them, and I like to see how a team's stopper [top relief pitcher] did if he came in." Adds Johnson, who also reads the box scores, "I like to see when a team used a particular relief pitcher."

While Harrelson studies his paper, Robinson, who also serves as the Mets' hitting instructor, determines the order in which his charges will take batting practice. This is not often as simple as it sounds. Three different coaches throw batting practice and many of the players have favorites. "Some of the guys are a little tempermental," says Robinson. "They only like to hit off a certain coach. So you have to maneuver a bit, blow a little smoke. Tell a player, "You don't care who's pitching, as good a hitter as you are."

When the Mets (and most other teams) are at home, they

use videotape to instruct struggling pitchers and hitters. The players will come in early to meet with Stottlemyre or Robinson and compare replays of themselves when they were going well with more recent tapes. Stottlemyre will also view tapes alone, "just to reassure myself that I'm not missing anything." This was the case earlier this year when Cy Young Award-winner Dwight Gooden was having a little difficulty on the mound. Critics argued that Gooden's delivery was off, but Stottlemyre disagreed. Several trips to the VCR later, Stottlemyre remained convinced there was nothing wrong with his star pitcher's mechanics.

Even players who aren't struggling use the tapes. Despite the fact that he is one of the best hitters in baseball, Keith Hernandez, the Mets' first baseman, is a frequent visitor to the videotape room. "He just likes to get refreshed in there," explains Stottlemyre. (Hernandez is also one of the players who might be seen before a game working on his bats, trying to get them just right. All clubhouses have a place where a player or equipment man can sand the handle of a bat so that it feels more comfortable or make other adjustments. Hernandez also frequently asks trainers Garland and Sikes to take alcohol and remove some of the pine tar from his bat.)

In New York, Robinson may also order extra batting practice in Shea Stadium's batting cage for those who are slumping. "I like working in the [indoor] cage as opposed to on the field because you can go one-on-one with a player," says Robinson. "I can close the door, holler and kick him in the butt if I have to." Robinson doesn't like to "mess with a guy" unless the player is at his nadir. "When you're going good, I stay away. You don't need me. When you're going bad, you're much more open to constructive criticism," the coach says. This season Robinson has concentrated on helping veteran third baseman Ray Knight return to the excellent form he displayed several years ago. "Ray was too crouched, bent way over. He wasn't utilizing his God-given ability—strong hands," says Robinson. "We worked a lot and

I told him point-blank, "If you don't change, you're gonna lose your job." The result? Knight has hit well and kept his job.

Unfortunately, on the road, particularly before a day game, there is no time for individualized instruction, no time for anything other than the batting practice a fan can see if he or she comes to the park early. National League rules mandate 40 minutes of batting practice for the visiting club. "Not nearly enough," complains Robinson, who says he has worked out "gentlemen's agreements" with several other hitting instructors. "I give them an hour when they're in New York, if they'll give me an hour," he explains. All the Mets' pitchers also take batting practice when the team is at home. The group bunts for 15 minutes, then swings away for another quarter of an hour. "So when you see a pitcher fail on a bunt attempt in a game, don't think it's because he hasn't practiced," says Hoscheit.

On the road, the only pitcher to hit is the day's starter. Robinson puts that man, Ron Darling, with four of the Mets' reserves in "Group One: 12:50 to 1:03." Five other players, mostly starting players, comprise "Group Two: 1:03 to 1:16." And "Group Three: 1:16 to 1:30" is made up of players Robinson terms "the big boys." These are the team's better hitters, its stars, and Robinson lets them hit last because "they've earned the right to stay in the clubhouse and relax a little longer." Today the big boys are Gary Carter, George Foster (whom the Mets later released), Knight, Darryl Strawberry, and Hernandez.

A look around the locker room reveals that all are in attendance. Catcher Carter has just emerged from the trainer's room, his first stop in any ball park. Having undergone three operations on his left knee, he requires extensive pregame taping. In addition to all the catching gear you see him wearing, he has both ankles taped and wears from left ankle to thigh a prewrapped bandage and tape to protect the knee. Unlike adhesive tape, the prewrap gives the bum knee some give. "It's almost like getting additional tendons, but it takes about half an hour of taping before I can even put my uniform on," says Carter.

Hernandez, who also has his tender ankles taped each day, works a crossword puzzle. "What's one of the four horsemen of the Apocalypse, five letters?" he asks no one in particular. Strawberry reviews the scouting reports. "I'm interested in knowing about their hitters so I can position myself," says the right fielder. Foster is riding the exercise bicycle in the locker room, while Knight kibbitzes around the cards and dominos tables. The Mets players, like those on virtually every team, are chronic games players (backgammon is another favorite). "It relaxes you before a game," explains Strawberry. The stakes in the hearts and gin games are usually steaks or some other dinner on the town, while the dominos games, with players moving in and out quickly, are played for clubhouse bragging rights.

Relaxation is certainly a prevailing theme in the hours well before a game. Ball players can often be found in front of the clubhouse television set . . . today the Mets have seen both wrestling and Wimbledon tennis; the California Angels rarely miss "The People's Court"; the Seattle Mariners groove to "American Bandstand"; answering letters; signing baseball after baseball (generally used by the club for charitable or promotional purposes); or reading the box scores (rarely will you see a player reading a book in the clubhouse).

Because of the recent drug scandals, outsiders other than the press are generally not admitted to the clubhouse. An exception seems to be the omnipresent sports equipment representative, be it someone filling orders for Adidas or Nike or, as is the case today, a salesman for Rawlings, a major manufacturer of baseball gloves. Harrelson and infielders Howard Johnson and Wally Backman sample his wares, which, if chosen, will be complimentary.

Not everyone in the clubhouse is taking it easy. The training room is now populated by a number of pitchers doing their daily exercise and stretching routines. Says Garland, "Pitching is so traumatic for the arm that we like our pitchers to strengthen their rotator cuffs [near the shoulder]." Garland takes the hurlers through range-of-motion exercises, and they do their own workouts with hand-held dumbbells weighing two to five pounds. Home team locker rooms are more elaborate than those of the visitors. In Wrigley Field, the Cubs have a special workout room with various modern machines, while the Mets have one exercise bicycle. When at home, several Mets pitchers and position players use the Cybex and Nautilus weight machines either for overall conditioning or to strengthen specific weaknesses—Carter works on his knee, for example; pitcher Sid Fernandez works on his shoulder.

Manager Johnson likes to work out when he gets to the ball park, then take it easy before game time. But he has his game face on when he gets to the park. Although the Mets are already well in front of their division on this late June day, Johnson does not look like someone who stops and smells the roses. He is a man on a mission. The distance between each point he makes to the sportswriters is one straight line. This air of intensity hangs over the clubhouse—perhaps more so than those of other teams, be they contenders or also-rans. While most managers hold a formal staff meeting before each new series to go over scouting reports and personnel, Johnson doesn't. "Most of our meetings are in bars," laughs Harrelson. "I talk to the coaches and the players," Johnson says, not laughing. "The pitching coach and the hitting coach don't do anything without my knowledge."

One person Johnson does not talk to on game day is his starting pitcher. One might think the manager would want to give this crucial participant either a word of instruction or encouragement but, says Johnson, "He's got other things to do. He doesn't need to talk to me."

Actually, Darling, today's starter, is not particularly busy at the moment; he is helping Hernandez with the crossword puzzle. The ex-Yale pitcher's day began with a light breakfast at the hotel. He will shortly have his ankles taped, then take batting practice, cool off in the dugout, return to the training room to stretch, and then warm up for the game in the bull pen. Most pitchers chart pitches the day before they are scheduled to start. That is, they sit in the dugout and record each pitch—type and location—thrown by their teammates in that day's game. Generally, such an exercise serves as excellent preparation for the next day's outing, for the pitcher is forced to pay attention to the opposing hitters and how they handle particular pitches. But because the right-handed Darling usually follows the left-handed Ojeda in the rotation, he often is watching several hitters whom he will not face (because managers like to have left-handed batters face right-handed pitchers and prefer right-handed batters to face left-handed pitchers). At any rate, the point is moot because yesterday's rainout left Darling without a game to chart.

Many pitchers will spend time before a game reviewing the scouting reports or books that they may keep themselves on the hitters. Many pitchers, too, will engage their catcher and pitching coach in discussion about how best to approach the opponent. Darling is an exception. On this day, he will have no formal conversation with Carter, and his dialogue with Stottlemyre will be limited to a discussion of only a few of the Cubs. "I'll refresh his memory if he had trouble with any of these guys the last time he faced them," says the pitching coach. "But otherwise I'll leave him alone until he starts to warm up." Indeed, Darling is so relaxed when it comes to making today's start that by the time he leaves the clubhouse for batting practice he has failed to even look at the Cubs' lineup card. Waiting for the Cubs to clear the field, he registers surprise when someone tells him that Davey Lopes rather than Ron Cey is starting at third base. (The lineup card has been posted by Hoscheit, of course. It details the Cubs' starting batting order and all reserves, noting whether a man bats left-handed or right-handed. It also lists all the Cubs pitchers, their delivery times, and whether they throw lefty or righty. The card is initially posted for all to see in the clubhouse, then is moved to the dugout before the game. Hoscheit takes his own version of this down to the bull pen once the game begins so that his relief pitchers will be able to figure out whom they might be facing.)

By 12:45 all the Mets in batting practice Group One and most of their teammates, save a few of the big boys, are waiting impatiently for the field. But the time in the dugout is not necessarily wasted. Stottlemyre tries to watch the opposition take batting practice. "You can pick things up," he says. "Hitters can't hide how they hit a particular pitch. They'll usually hit it the same way in the game as they do in practice. I encourage my pitchers to watch, too." Fielders can also benefit. The New York Yankees' Dave Winfield, for example, studies opposing hitters during batting practice, trying to see how well they are hitting the ball and, more important, what they are trying to do at the plate. Are they trying to hit the ball up the middle? To the opposite field? Such observations will help him position himself in right field during the game.

At 12:50 the Cubs are done. Hoscheit announces, "Okay. Let's do it," and the army moves. To the fan who watches what follows it may seem that little of import is taking place, particularly away from the batting cage. But the hour that follows has actually been tightly choreographed, and almost every movement has a definite purpose. Watching all this is a little like watching a three-ring circus, for there is activity at the cage, in the infield, and in the outfield.

There is a difference of opinion in the Mets' camp about the purpose of batting practice, commonly called "BP." Says Harrelson, who is one of the coaches to pitch, "I like to see the guys hit it out of the park. I know when I was playing, it was a big confidence booster. No one likes to come away thinking, 'Gee, I couldn't even hit one out in BP.' That's my thinking. But then I'm not the hitting instructor."

And what is the thinking of the hitting instructor? "I don't like to see the guys try for home runs all the time," says Robinson. "Batting practice is a time to work on your timing, hit the ball to the opposite field. When I played for [manager]

Ralph Houk with the Yankees, he'd call BP off if the guys were hitting too many. Home runs come when you least expect them."

Strawberry speaks for most of the Mets' hitters when he agrees with Robinson. "I take BP very seriously. I use it to get my swing down. I don't try to hit the long ball. I work on my line-drive stroke."

The fan who watches a team like the Mets that takes batting practice seriously should be able to see a pattern emerge. Each hitter in a group is allotted a certain number of swings. When the group has completed a cycle of swings, it starts over, continuing until its time is up. When a batter enters the box, he does not start swinging. Hoscheit details the procedure: On the first pitch, the batter pretends he is sacrificing and bunts. Then he pretends there's a runner on second base and he must advance him (so righties try to go the opposite way, hit to the right side of the field, and lefties try to pull the ball). Then the batter pretends the runner has reached third and the batter has to drive him in with a long fly ball. Says Hoscheit, "Fans don't realize it, but the better hitters are always pretending there's a game situation. I'll stand at the cage and hear batters say things like, 'Two outs, bases loaded, gotta hit a line drive,' and then I'll see them swing down on the ball to hit it straight rather than come up on it to hit a fly ball." Sure enough, when Knight comes up he calls out exactly what he is trying to execute, "Sacrifice. Hit and run. Sac fly." When a hitter gets done with his first round of swings, he continues his imaginary game, running the bases as if the next man at the plate were bunting, then executing the hit and run.

If Harrelson and Robinson have different ideas about hitting home runs in batting practice, they agree that you cannot predict how well a player will perform in the game based on the number of home runs, line drives, or weak ground balls he hits in BP. Carter also agrees. "There are some days when I have a bad BP then have a great game and vice versa. You can't tell," he says.

While his hitters are taking batting practice, Robinson is in one of two places—either behind the batting cage observing and making pertinent suggestions or down one of the foul lines hitting "fungoes" to his outfielders. Fungoes, which are hit with a special bat that is flat on one side, are simply fly balls hit in practice so that a fielder can get loose and test the conditions in the ball park. At Wrigley Field, both the sun and the wind can be treacherous.

"The first thing a coach or player does when he comes out is check the elements," says Harrelson. "You look at the flags, see how the wind is blowing, check the field." When Harrelson managed in the minor leagues at Little Falls, New York, he noticed that at the same time every day the sun was in such a position that the third baseman was completely blinded. "You bet I took advantage of that," he remembers. "If we had a runner on second base, I don't care how slow he was, I'd have him steal, because I knew there was no way the third baseman could see the ball." Today Harrelson wants to determine if the recent rain has slowed the infield. "If it has, I might tell a guy that he can take an extra base on an outfielder or that he might be able to bunt if the third baseman is playing back because the wet grass will slow down the ball."

Harrelson pitches batting practice to Group Three, the big boys. But he has other duties as well. While Group One and Two take BP, he hits ground balls to the Mets' infielders, who have assumed their positions in the field. As the chapter on fielding indicates, infielders and outfielders take this time seriously. Says veteran shortstop Rafael Santana, "If you don't, you get into bad habits." Santana, like most other fielders, uses the time to loosen up, get his timing down, and, if need be, work on particular aspects of his defense, like charging ground balls or turning the double play. (This is not the only opportunity he'll get before the game. After batting practice is over, the fielders engage in a more formal infield practice.)

When Group Three is ready to hit, Harrelson assumes the mound. There is a real art to throwing batting practice.

Harrelson's approach: "I don't throw breaking balls because I'm trying to build confidence, but I do try and move the ball around. The big thing is to maintain speed. The guys like it thrown harder rather than softer because they know they'll see more hard pitches in a game. They want to get a feel for the speed of the game." Throwing hard BP day after day can take its toll on an arm. "I had some pains of popping and cracking at first, but knock on wood, my arm has been sound," says Harrelson. Former Red Sox coach Walt Hriniak has not been so fortunate. Over the last several years, he has required several operations on his shoulder and elbow.

By the time the big boys are in the cage, manager Johnson has moved to a protective screen that sits on the edge of the outfield grass behind second base. He talks with Stottlemyre and Hoscheit. He does not talk to members of the Cubs who have stayed around the batting cage and on the sidelines. "I don't believe in fraternization," says Johnson. "I frown on my players talking to guys on the other team, but I don't have a rule." This extreme attitude is the exception, not the rule in baseball, although it does have some adherents. The Minnesota Twins' outstanding reliever Jeff Reardon won't talk with opponents because he feels the less a hitter knows about him, the better. Coach Harrelson's philosophy is more the norm: "I think fraternization is healthy, but not if it's gonna cost. Not if you're not paying attention to what you're supposed to be doing. The game is serious, but you gotta have fun." Actually, there is a league regulation prohibiting fraternization, and when the umpires arrive at the ball park about an hour and 15 minutes before game time, the man who was behind the plate the previous evening sits in the stands behind home plate, still in his street clothes. "If we see two guys from opposite clubs talking, we're supposed to warn them to stop," explains veteran umpire John Kibler. "If they refuse, then we're supposed to report them to the league, which will fine them." Understandably, the umpires are rather lax in their enforcement. "You don't want to get a guy mad at you before the game even starts," says Kibler.

While the hitters and fielders prepare for the game, the pitchers are equally busy. Stottlemyre is a believer in the saying, "A pitcher is only as strong as his legs." The Mets' pitchers (except for the game's starter) keep their legs strong by shagging fly balls during batting practice and by running in the outfield. Stottlemyre has two different running drills. He either stands amid his hurlers and throws them the ball (like a quarterback to a receiver) as they sprint by or, as is the case today, he simply orders them to run a certain number of sprints along the outfield wall. Today the starters will run 12 to 14 80-yard sprints, while the relief pitchers run eight to 10 sprints. The short relievers may not run as many as the middle relievers. Why? "They see more action and we don't want to tire them out," explains Hoscheit.

Stottlemyre takes a catcher's mitt to the visitor's bull pen and warms up Ojeda in accordance with the earlier discussion with Johnson. Not every pitching coach actually catches his starters, but says Stottlemyre, "I like to warm them up myself so I can monitor them. I can control how much they throw, see how their stuff is, and if they're working on something new, I can get a first-hand view."

The Mets, like most teams today, have a five-man rotation, meaning, not counting open dates and postponements, the starters take the mound after four days' rest. Here, according to Hoscheit, is what they do in between starts: "On Day One, they don't do much of anything but run. (Darling is an exception. He likes to throw the day after to get the blood flowing in his pitching arm right away.) On Day Two, they throw for about 10 to 15 minutes, maybe working on new pitches, too. On Day Three, they mostly run. They may play a little catch on the side. And on Day Four, they run, play a little catch, and they also have to pick up balls during batting practice." He smiles, then adds, "They hate picking up the balls." Superstars are not exempt. Gooden is scheduled to pitch tomorrow. He comes out of the dugout and plays a light game of catch with relief pitcher Doug Sisk for a few minutes, then begins his custodial duties.

Unlike starters, relief pitchers rarely throw before a game begins. This is because they usually get plenty of work warming up in the bull pen during a game in anticipation of taking the mound, if not pitching in the game itself. One of the things Stottlemyre and Johnson discuss in their pregame meeting is which relievers need additional work. Those relievers who haven't warmed up or pitched for a couple of days will throw while the game is in progress so they won't get too rusty.

Fielding practice follows batting practice. While the infielders take ground balls, Robinson and other Mets' coaches continue to hit balls to the outfielders. A special effort is made to hit the ball into the outfield corners or against the wall so left fielder Foster and right fielder Strawberry can judge the angles of bounces and bumps. Some of the pitchers also come out and field balls hit from close range.

While all this is going on the umpires are readying themselves. They keep their distance from the players and coaches. They have a separate dressing room at the park and almost always stay at a different hotel than the visitors. Today Kibler will be behind the plate. It is his responsibility to rub up five dozen official baseballs with a special mud provided by the league. It takes about 20 minutes. The other umpires read the sports section, paying special attention to any controversial plays in games played yesterday, discussing how they would handle similar situations. They wonder aloud whether on this muggy day they'll get the always-hoped-for "fast game."

Half an hour before game time, the Mets leave the field. Most of the players retreat to the clubhouse to relax, a handful stay in the dugout, and a few stretch or do a little extra running on the sidelines. Starting pitcher Darling enters the trainer's room, where Sikes stretches the pitcher's legs and his right shoulder. "By loosening up his pitching arm, we can save him about 30 to 35 warm-up pitches," explains Garland.

When the stretching is over, Darling picks up a jacket and a towel and heads for the bull pen. He begins his final tuneup by playing catch for three or four minutes with bull pen catcher John Malkin. Then he moves to the bull pen mound and begins throwing, relatively slowly and softly at first, harder as the clock ticks the minutes to game time. Stottlemyre stands over his shoulder, reminding him about certain Cub hitters and checking his mechanics. Most starters like to throw for 15 minutes before the game starts, throwing about six pitches a minute. Darling likes to throw for 20 minutes, so he will throw well over 100 pitches before he even faces an opponent. Darling is also unique on the staff in that he likes to warm up with a "batter" standing at the plate. Coach Robinson plays the role of opponent, standing batless on the right, then the left, so Darling can get a better feel for the strike zone.

Darling throws to Malkin for the first 10 minutes and then to reserve catcher, Ed Hearn. Again, the Mets waste no motion. Playing behind All-Star Carter, Hearn sees very little action. (He was eventually traded.) He therefore uses the warm-up period to familiarize himself with the Mets' pitchers. Darling's pitches to Hearn, particularly in the final few minutes, seem to have more zip. Explains Stottlemyre, "As time winds down, I tell my pitcher to pretend that he's actually pitching to the first few hitters he'll face. That way he's got a better chance of being ready when the game begins."

Darling looks sharp. But just as batting practice is no predictor of what will happen once the umpire calls, "Play ball," neither is the pitcher's warm-up. Says Hoscheit, "I remember when Catfish Hunter was at Oakland. Sometimes he'd look so lousy warming up, I'd call our manager and say, 'The Cat don't have it today.' And then he'd go out and pitch a one-hit shutout. Then other times he'd look perfect warming up and he'd struggle all day long. All a coach can tell a manager is, 'It looks like we may have trouble.' "

At 2:20 Kibler and his crew meet with Cubs coach John Vukovich and Mets coach Bill Robinson and receive the starting lineups. If there had been any beanball incidents in the clubs' most recent series, the umpires might warn each team that the first time a pitcher intentionally throws at a batter he will be ejected. Despite a minor history of beanball wars in past years, the Mets and Cubs do not, based on their competition this season, require that lecture. The umps do, however, ask Robinson if he needs to be reminded of any Wrigley Field ground rules. For example, if a ball gets stuck in the ivy on the outfield walls, play stops if the outfielder chasing the ball indicates it is lost or tangled in the vines. The umpires then decide how many bases to award the batter and any runners who may have been on base. However, if the outfielder doesn't quit the chase and begins digging for the ball, play continues, even if he can't find it.

Darling is now in the dugout. Kibler calls "Play ball." And we can finally see the fruits of all the preparation that has taken place since Hoscheit arrived at the park.

POSTSCRIPT: On this day, Darling took his good stuff from the bull pen to the mound. Although Lopes, whose insertion into the lineup surprised the pitcher, got three hits, Darling allowed the Cubs only two runs in seven strong innings. The Mets won 5-2, scoring three runs in the 9th inning. The renewed Knight knocked in the game-winning run with a single. By day's end the Mets were in first place in the National League East, an impressive 9 1/2 games ahead of the second-place Expos. If manager Johnson, who seemed to be pushing all the right buttons, was smiling, it was behind closed doors. The season, the mission, had a long way to go.

2
PITCHING:
THE HEART OF THE GAME

We pitchers play a different game than all the other guys for one reason: we get charged with the win or loss.
—Billy Muffett, Detroit Tigers pitching coach

The big yellow pad was filled before the 1986 season was three weeks old. On it, Sparky Anderson had written the Detroit Tigers' schedule from May 1 to October 5. Opposite each date was the name of the pitcher whom the veteran manager expected to take the mound for his ball club. Asked who would be playing what position in the field or hitting in which spot in his batting order as early as next week, Anderson acknowledged that he was uncertain. "But the pitching is set," he said firmly. "Pitching is the most important thing in baseball."

But wasn't this supposed to be the year of the hitter, Sparky? Look at the talented bats in your division alone: Wade Boggs and the rest of the Red Sox; Jesse Barfield and the Blue Jays; Don Mattingly and company in New York; Eddie Murray and the Orioles; even Cleveland has some solid hitters; not to mention your own powerful lineup.

"How many clubs have you seen win the division with just sheer power?" Anderson retorted. "I haven't seen too many.

They may finish second or third, but they don't win it all very often."

He was right. Only once in the last nine years—1982—had the American League East winner not led the division in earned run average. When the Tigers ran away with the championship in 1984, their pitching staff was tops in the league. In 1985, however, the staff posted only the third best ERA in the division, and the team fell to third place.

The names that Anderson had written in on his pad were familiar and impressive. There was fireballer Jack Morris, the 1980s winningest pitcher. Frank Tanana, once a flamethrower but now a finesse pitcher, who won 10 games for the Tigers in 1985 after coming over from Texas in late June. Dan Petry, thought by many to be on the verge of superstardom, and the only pitcher in baseball other than Morris to win 15 games in each of the last four years. Walt Terrell, late of the Mets, and 15-10 in 1985, his first year with the Tigers. And Dave LaPoint, a winner with the Cardinals for several years, but a hard-luck loser with the Giants in 1985, who hoped to find new life in Detroit.

"This staff has the potential to be one of the better ones in baseball," Anderson said as the season began. But by the middle of May, the yellow pad had been rendered inoperative by injuries (Petry was lost with a bad elbow) and ineffectiveness (LaPoint never regained his groove). By the All-Star break, the Tigers, favored by many to win their division because of the superiority of their pitching were, for the first time since divisional play began in 1969, dead last. Who led the league at the halfway mark? Boston. Why? Because the team's perennially powerful hitters were now complemented by the best pitching staff in the American League.

Then the Red Sox pitchers began to experience trouble and the Tigers hurlers came to life. Morris, the spiritual leader as well as the ace of the staff had given up a home run on his very first pitch of the season . . . and things had gone downhill from there. Now, however, he was back on track, pitching three shutouts in a row. Terrell, who had started strong but faded, returned to form. And rookie Eric King picked up the slack for Petry and LaPoint, who was eventually traded to the San Diego Padres. The Tigers, thanks to good pitching and Boston's lack of same, were quickly back in the championship race. Finally, another turnaround. The Red Sox pitchers, led by Roger Clemens, revived, and Boston took the division. The two clubs were on top of the A.L. East the next two seasons. In 1987, the Tigers, behind a strong starting staff, took division honors. But in 1988, the Red Sox, riding the arms of Clemens, Bruce Hurst, and Lee Smith, triumphed. "No doubt about it," says Ken "Hawk" Harrelson, former Chicago White Sox executive vice president for baseball operations, "pitching is the heart and lungs of baseball."

It might appear that watching the pitcher and understanding what he is trying to do is the easiest part of watching a baseball game. Our eyes are automatically drawn to the man with the ball; we follow his delivery and immediately know the result of his effort—strike, ball, hit, out. But there is much more we can watch for—the pitcher's demeanor, his level of confidence, competitiveness, and concentration; the rapport between pitcher and catcher; the mechanics of the pitcher's delivery (the Tigers' Muffett, for example, insists that the well-trained eye focused on, of all things, the pitcher's belt, can provide a clue as to how well the man is doing); and perhaps most interesting, the pitcher's style, his ball's velocity and movement, his pitch selection and location.

Velocity. Movement. Pitch selection. Location. A brief primer is in order. Pitchers throw any number of different pitches. The fastball, the curveball, slider, and change-up are most common, and they may be supplemented by variations such as the increasingly popular split-fingered fastball, the forkball, palm ball, screwball, knuckleball, and others. (All these pitches are described in greater detail at the end of this chapter.) The fastball is the pitch relied upon most heavily by most pitchers. The top pitchers—the Red Sox's Clemens, the Mets' Dwight Gooden, for example—can throw the ball at upward of 95 miles per hour, while mere mortal pitchers generate speeds of more than 90 mph. Power pitchers often use the fastball to set up the other pitches they throw. The difference in the velocity and movement of these other pitches—they are obviously slower and approach the plate following a less direct route—is what keeps the hitter off guard, particularly if he is guessing that a particular pitch is on the way and the pitcher crosses him up. But while speed is important (as television announcers who constantly refer to the velocity of a radar-gun-measured fastball remind us), unless a fastball has movement—that is, it rises or falls or tails in or out as it approaches the plate—the best batters will eventually be able to hit it. And even if the fastball does have movement, there are few if any pitchers who succeed in the game if the fastball is all they can throw. They need other pitches because the better hitters are masters of adjusting. If they know that a pitcher is going to rely solely on a fastball, they can time their swings accordingly. Gooden and the Houston Astros' Nolan Ryan, for example, are such devastating pitchers not only because they have overpowering fastballs, but because they have a great curveball to go with the fastball.

As important as what pitch is thrown is *where* the pitch is thrown—inside, outside, up or down, in the strike zone or intentionally wasted out of the strike zone. Why would a pitcher try to throw a pitch out of the strike zone? Either to entice a batter to swing at a bad, less hittable pitch; to move the batter away from the plate (moving him away will make it more difficult for him to reach future pitches on the outside of the plate; this is accomplished by a fastball up and inside); or to set up a particular pitch that will soon follow (get the batter's timing off by throwing him an out-of-the-strike-zone slow curve or change-up and then come back on the next pitch with the fastball).

Of course, if a pitcher is to have the luxury of being able to waste pitches out of the strike zone, he must have the control to put the ball in the strike zone. Wasted pitches usually come when the pitcher is ahead in the count, in no immediate danger of giving the hitter that most hated of happenings, a walk. Why is the walk anathema to almost every pitcher? "If I can keep runners off the bases, a lot less bad things can happen," says Petry, later traded to the California Angels. "I figure if I can keep down the number of walks I give, everything else—wins and earned run average—will take care of itself."

Statistics show that a pitcher is much more likely to issue a walk if his first pitch to a batter is a ball. This suggests one of the most important principles of pitching, simply articulated by Muffett: "Everyone knows there ain't but one way to pitch, and that's being ahead in the count."

Although a pitcher will almost always try to throw a strike on his first pitch to a particular batter, rarely will he throw the same pitch in the same location to the same batter during a game. While you may not be able to see that a pitch is a mere, but telling, couple of inches away from an earlier one, you can see what the general location is by watching where the catcher sets up his target—inside or outside, up or down—and where the pitch ends up. Go one step further and note what the count is when particular locations are sought and you have added another layer to your awareness.

If a pitcher does try to throw the same pitch to a batter too many times, he may be courting disaster. Says former Cy Young Award-winner Steve Stone, "Let's say a pitcher has gotten a hitter out two straight times on a fastball inside. He's shown him how he wants to get him out. This is a trap that starting pitchers sometimes fall into. Now the same batter comes up with the bases loaded. The pitcher tries to come inside one more time. Well, if the hitter has any intelligence—which they do—he opens up [his stance so he can hit the inside pitch] quickly and he doubles to the opposite field. The pitcher wonders, 'How'd he hit that pitch?' But you showed him, say, with nobody on base and two out in the 2nd inning and again with nobody on and one out in the 5th inning that you're gonna get him out by pitching inside. You haven't saved the spot for when you need it, bases loaded in the 8th inning. You've gone to his weakness twice, now when you go that third time, look out."

The same week that Stone, now a commentator for the Chicago Cubs, spoke these words, the Kansas City Royals' Frank White hit a home run late in the game to power his team past the Minnesota Twins. When asked how he did it, White explained that the Twins' pitchers had started him off with a fastball inside on each of his previous at bats, so he guessed that that would be the pitch he'd see once again. He did!

While most pitchers feel confident that they can beat most hitters with their fastball most of the time, it takes confidence to use their other pitches when that becomes necessary. Listen to Dan Petry: "I used to be primarily a fastball and slider pitcher, but over the years I developed a change-up and curveball. Now I feel I can throw all four of them. I hope having the off-speed pitches to go along with the hard stuff will make me a lot more successful. I developed the new pitches through hard work. Just throwing them over and over again until they finally felt good. It takes confidence to use them in game situations. A lot of times you grip a certain pitch and you think, 'I don't know if I'm going to throw this over the screen, out of the stadium, or what.' You have no idea where it's going. It takes a lot of time to where when you're winding up you feel good about it—think that it's going over the plate, do what it's supposed to do."

Ask any manager to list what he's looking for in a pitcher and "confidence" will be close to the top of his list. Says Petry, "Every pitcher has talent or he wouldn't be in the big leagues. So the mental part of the game really comes into play. When I say 'mental,' I really mean 'confidence'—just believing you can get the hitter out."

Getting the hitter out. Consider what is involved: before each pitch, the man on the mound (with help from his catcher) must evaluate the situation in the game—the number of outs, the position of any runners on base and the likelihood that they might try to steal, the known strengths and weaknesses of the batter, the known strengths and weaknesses of the batters to follow, his own strengths and weaknesses. All this just to decide *what* pitch to throw and where to throw it. That decision made—and it has to be made in but a few seconds—he then must go into his delivery. Now he must concentrate on being mechanically correct (more about mechanics later), must pay attention to any runners on base, must hide the ball so he won't tip the pitch to an alert batter, coach, or base runner. If he makes a mistake it could cost his team the ball game. If he does everything right, the pitch should land within two inches of the desired location. But wait! That's assuming the hitter just stands there and watches the pitch go by. If the batter swings, the pitch must be good enough so that he misses or at least doesn't hit it how and where he wants to hit it. Consider, too, that all this is done in front of thousands or even millions more watching on television. Are pitchers aware of this? "Yes," says Morris. "You hear the fans cheering and booing, trying to affect everything you're doing. You've gotta turn that off and throw it."

Hitters, of course, must go through a parallel exercise on each pitch. But the pressure is different. "I think you have to have a lot more confidence to be a pitcher," says LaPoint. "You go out there and you really have to take charge. From pitch 1 to pitch 100 you have to know what you're doing every pitch. A batter can take a bad swing and maybe foul off the ball or maybe he makes an out the first time up and then maybe hits a home run the next time. He's got four or five chances every game. But the pitcher—you throw one bad pitch and there's a chance you may be out of the game."

Even if a hitter fails to redeem himself after a bad at bat, he can redeem himself in the field. And even if he has an entire bad game at the plate, there is always tomorrow. Not so the starting pitcher. Says Anderson, "Think of the pressure of being a starting pitcher who only gets to go out there every fourth or fifth day. If you're playing every day and go oh for four, you know you can get right back at it tomorrow. But if a starter doesn't do well, he has to think about it for three or four days before he can do anything. So some pitchers look like they're in a state of depression and others seem to be hyper."

Neither hyperactivity nor depression is apparent in the demeanor of the game's more confident pitchers. You don't necessarily have to know baseball to judge such character. It is evident in the way these men conduct themselves on the mound and in the way they challenge hitters. Look into Morris's eyes when he's pitching and you see the modern-day equivalent of William Blake's "Tiger, Tiger." "You have to believe in yourself," he says. "There are times when I go out there and say to myself, 'Even though I don't have my best stuff, I know I can beat this team.' I have to admit I'm quite cocky in this regard, but you have to be. That's the approach you have to take because the game is so competitive, so well-balanced that to me the winning edge is what you have in your heart." Many pitchers play a guessing game with the hitter—can I throw something he's not expecting?—but Morris generally is willing to match his strength against the hitter's strength. "I want to know if a guy is a better off-speed or fastball hitter," he says, "but a lot of times I'm going to go with my best against his best. There's more of a guessing game when you have less confidence in yourself. You think, 'Maybe I shouldn't throw that because he's better than I am at that particular pitch.' A lot of times, however, when you're confident and strong—and I've been in those situations—it just doesn't matter."

Opposing hitters aren't the only ones to feel the heat of Morris's competitive fires. "If I see one of our pitchers isn't challenging a hitter he ought to be challenging, giving him too much credit for something he doesn't deserve, I'll tell him, 'C'mon, go after him. If he hits it out, he hits it out,' " says Morris.

Even the manager is not immune. Morris recalls a game in which Anderson came to the mound and, indicating he was thinking about bringing in a relief pitcher, asked him how he felt. "After the game, I told him, 'Sparky, don't ever ask me that question again. You're the manager of this team. It's your decision to make. You've got to analyze what I'm doing. If you think I'm done, then you get me out of there. But I'm never gonna tell you I feel terrible. I'm gonna tell you I feel fine. That's just the way I am.'"

Anderson remembers the episode and laughs. "If you didn't know Jack Morris off the field, you'd think he was a pretty nasty guy from the way he acts on the field. But he just wants to win so badly."

As badly as a pitcher wants to win, he can't let his competitiveness overwhelm his powers of concentration (early in his career Morris had a tendency to let this happen). Says Stone, "As a starter you'll go to the mound 35 times a year and there may be seven to 10 times when you're enchanted—you've got great stuff—and it's not hard to win on those days because you look at the outside corner of the plate and the catcher calls for the curveball and you throw it right in his glove. But what separates the men from the boys is the ability to win with less than your good stuff. The pitchers with the good concentration, those are the guys that can overcome adversity when they're 60 to 70 percent effective."

Stone is adept at spotting concentration lapses. His secret? "I like to watch the pitcher's eyes because I can tell when he loses concentration. And when that happens, I know he's not long for the game."

Like Morris, Stone was a competitor. Some pitchers rely totally on their catchers to call the pitches. (Says LaPoint, who falls into this category, "I don't think I have the experience to call my own game.") But others, Stone among them, insist on the final say. Stone always told his catcher, "As soon as you see a column that says, 'Losing Catcher,' I'll let you control the game. Until then, I will."

Still, Stone acknowledges the need for rapport between pitcher and catcher. "Watch the confidence the catcher expresses to his pitcher," he advises the fan. "And watch the pitcher tip you off to whether he has confidence in the catcher by his attitude toward him. Whether he's indicating, 'Get be-hind the plate and don't bother me,' or he's really working with the catcher."

The catcher and pitcher are called the battery, and when they are working together they can provide a team with an important charge. "I say it jokingly but it's true: what a pitcher and catcher are really doing is playing catch," says Muffett. "If they can get the rhythm flowing, get in a groove, you won't have any trouble."

Adds veteran pitcher Tommy John, who is approaching 300 victories, "For me or any pitcher, a catcher is absolutely vital. I like to delegate authority. If you have a good catcher, you go over the game plan of how you want to pitch and then delegate that authority to the man behind the plate. He can see things the pitcher can't see—watch the batter's feet, watch if the batter is diving after pitches. The catcher can tell me if we've got to come inside more, change speeds more. A lot of times the pitcher can't tell this. A good pitcher and catcher are like a hand and glove. If it's a nice fit, it's a tough combination to beat."

The development of the "game plan" John speaks of usual-ly begins prior to a series with an opponent, when the pitchers, coaches, and catchers go over scouting reports, which indicate the recent strengths and weaknesses of the opposing hitters. (Some pitchers and catchers actually keep their own books indicating their successes and failures with particular hitters). Then, the night before he is to pitch, a pitcher will review the lineup he expects to face. Says Petry, "You go over every hitter and try not to think about the times they've hit a home run or they've hit the ball hard off you, but think about the times when you've struck them out or made them pop up and how you did that. It's all memory."

John went one step beyond memorization, however. After going over the box scores to see which opposing players were hot, who was likely to steal and who was likely to hit and run, he would, as he puts it, "mentally pitch a game to the hitters, determining what I wanted to do. I'm a big believer in visualization. I'd visualize what I wanted to do to a hitter. Every time I threw a pitch in my mind, it was a good pitch. I think that makes the chances of making the pitch in the game much better." (It should be noted there are some pitchers who don't spend the night before a game doing their homework and are none the worse for it. Morris is a prime example. "I don't even like to think about the game at all until I go out to the bull pen to warm up, because I think a lot of energy is taken away from the concentration level I have to attain during the game. If I'm thinking about the hitters all day long, then I've forgotten what I have to do by the time I actually face them," he explains.).

Catcher Lance Parrish, an All Star with the Tigers and then the Philadelphia Phillies, like John and Petry, does do his homework in advance of the contest. And how does he go about calling pitches once the game begins? "I pretty much just make suggestions," he says philosophically. "If a pitcher wants to throw what I suggest—great. But pitchers are often in different moods. So I may call a game for a guy once and he may hardly ever shake me off (say no to the call). Then the next time he'll shake me off a lot more. When they're in different moods, they may want to throw a different ball game. I can't read their minds. If they don't like my suggestion, then they don't have to throw it. On the other hand, there are days when it's almost eerie. A guy will go with me the whole way. That makes my job a whole lot more enjoyable."

It makes it more enjoyable for the pitcher, too. "Sometimes it's spooky," says Walt Terrell. "There are days when I'll start to wind up before the catcher has even given me the sign because I know he's gonna call what I want to throw."

Calling pitches isn't the only service a good catcher can provide. Blocking pitches in the dirt not only prevents runners from advancing, but also gives the pitcher the confidence to throw the kind of pitches that might break downward. Throwing out base stealers gives the pitcher another luxury. Explains Muffett: "If you know your catcher has a good arm, then you can concentrate on the man at the plate and not worry so much about the runners." Good catchers also help out by "framing" pitches. That is, they catch a pitch that is close to the strike zone with their mitt positioned in such a way that the ball appears to be in the strike zone, or they literally bring the ball into the strike zone with a subtle move of the mitt. (The fan who watches closely should be able to see such chicanery.)

Parrish is one of the most skilled at all the above and at spotting flaws in the pitcher's mechanics, the elements of his delivery motion. As important as confidence, competitiveness, and concentration are, the pitcher who is not throwing the ball properly will have a much more difficult time of it than the pitcher with good mechanics. Muffett states another pitching principle: "If you have good mechanics, then you're going to be able to throw strikes."

The Los Angeles Dodgers' outstanding pitcher, John Tudor, is the first to agree. Traded by the Pittsburgh Pirates to the Cardinals prior to 1985, Tudor began that season by winning one game and losing seven. "I just couldn't figure out what was wrong," he remembers, "but then a friend from home, Dave Bettencourt, mentioned he'd seen a flaw in my motion. I should have a little hesitation in the middle of my delivery, and I wasn't doing it. What that did was make my arm late and throw my control off."

Can such a tiny thing throw off a pitcher's whole game? "I think so," says Tudor. "It's a routine, like anything else. You can't write with a pen between your last two fingers. When you form a routine, everything falls into that sequence. When you get up in the morning, you may walk with your right leg first, and if you get up and happen to walk with your left leg first it feels funny. It's the same thing in pitching mechanics. All it takes is one thing to throw other things off." Tudor corrected the flaw. His record the remainder of the season, as he helped lead the Cardinals to the World Series: 20 wins and one loss.

It is not the purpose of this book to get into a lengthy discussion on the mechanics of pitching. (Tom Seaver's wonderful book, *The Art of Pitching*, is an excellent source for those who want to know more.) However, the conscientious fan may find it fun to analyze the motion of the man on the mound and to prescribe from his or her seat in the stands the same solution that catcher Parrish or pitching coach Muffett or friend Bettencourt might offer.

The first step in becoming an analyst, says Muffett, is to realize that "mechanics are what a guy is capable of himself. There are basics that all pitchers have to do, but one guy might throw over the top, one might throw from the side, one might throw from underneath. So you have to watch each guy and figure out his mechanics. I ask my pitchers to tell me when they feel they're throwing well, so I can study them. Naturally, when you're going good, your mechanics are perfect."

What are some of the basics? Explains Muffett: "When you get ready to explode, go toward home, everything you're doing is going straight toward that plate. I don't want my legs to all of a sudden jump off the rubber or push back. I want everything I have going toward the plate. I want to be under control and have good balance. And just about the time I feel my weight is shifting toward the plate, I want my arm to be coming through at its maximum rate of speed. It's like in golf, where you want to get your club head through the ball."

Videotape can be helpful here. "But," says Terrell, "you have to have tapes of when you're going good and when you're bad. I've seen those tapes, and you can really tell there's a difference. When I was going bad, I was tilting my head back and my back was like a big bow. I was leaning back and not driving toward home plate, which caused my arm to be slow, and caused my pitches to be high."

Most hitters find high pitches the easiest to hit. Interestingly, in addition to being caused by the mechanical flaw described by Terrell, such pitches can also result if the pitcher is either too anxious or too tired. About anxiety, Muffett says, "When we get into trouble on the mound, our biggest tendency is to rush our delivery. When we do that, two things are happening together. We're getting out in front too quick, and our arms are dropping down. If the arm is down, the pitches have a tendency to be high or up in the strike zone." If a pitcher's arm is tired, it will also drop down, creating the same problem. That is why pitchers get in trouble as they get tired later in the game and why managers are so sensitive to the number of pitches a man has thrown.

From his spot next to Anderson on the bench, Muffett also watches how well his pitchers follow through (just as former Red Sox hitting coach Walt Hriniak watches his hitters for the same). Says Muffett: "Believe it or not, if a fan watches a pitcher's belt, he can tell how well a pitcher is throwing. Say with a right-hander, if his right hip is getting higher than his left hip at the belt area, then chances are he's going to be rounding out his shoulder and following through real well. Guys who throw with flat hips or a flat belt tend to throw the ball up more and get in trouble."

The shoulder is one of the first places Parrish looks, too, if a pitcher begins to experience trouble. "If the pitcher is rushing, he's probably opening up his front shoulder too quickly. If you watch closely, you'll see that this leads to dipping the throwing elbow, which leads to keeping the ball up in the strike zone or hanging a lot of breaking balls," he explains.

There are other reasons besides mechanics why a pitcher may struggle, particularly early in the game. Stone explains: "It's rhythm. Think about it. A football team, a kicker, warm up on the field they'll be playing on; a guy plays a practice round on the same golf course where the tournament is being held; a basketball team warms up at the hoop it will be shooting at. But a pitcher warms up in the bull pen, and once the game starts he'll never use that mound again. The mound on the field will be completely different. Mounds are like fingerprints—there are no two alike. So you've got to get used to it all over again.

"Your body has to get used to pitching, you have to get used to the flow of the game. A lot of pitchers don't get their rhythm early, and so they're vulnerable in the first and second and sometimes third inning. But then, with guys like [former Cardinals' great] Bob Gibson, Nolan Ryan—they never gave up a lead in the late innings. If you didn't get these guys early, you could mail in the results."

Curiously (or perhaps not so curiously), the discrepancy between the mound in the visitor's bull pen and the real mound is often greater than the discrepancy between the mound in the home team's bull pen and the real mound. Laughs Stone, "We all know the game is beyond reproach as far as integrity is concerned, but sometimes, perhaps, they [the home team's grounds crew] alter that mound in the visitor's bull pen. They might make it just a little higher. So what happens is that a guy might have a great curveball because that mound is higher (curveballs are more effective when thrown from a higher mound). But now he goes to the real mound and it's flat. And that great curveball stays up in the hitter's eyes for the first two innings [until the pitcher adjusts] and maybe someone hits it out of the park when he wouldn't have otherwise."

Just as different mounds may affect the battle between pitcher and hitter, so too might certain parks. The parks in the American League, have, in general, somewhat shorter dimensions than the parks in the National League. As a result, says Terrell, who has played in both leagues, "The American League parks favor high-ball hitters. If a batter gets the ball in the air in a lot of the American League parks [and this is more likely to happen if he gets a high pitch that he can get under], it's going to be a home run, where it might only be a long out in a National League Park." Do pitchers, therefore, tailor their styles to the park they're pitching in? They shouldn't, says Muffett. "You can't be pitching different in every town you go to. What we're looking for is consistency."

Adds Terrell: "I can't change my style because of the park I'm in. I'm gonna keep the ball low, whomever, wherever we're playing."

A pitcher like Terrell—in baseball parlance, he's a "control pitcher"—must keep the ball low because he doesn't have an overwhelming fastball. Thus a hitter might be able to get around on that pitch and hit it with authority. On the other hand, a Jack Morris—he's deemed a "power pitcher"—might be able to get away with keeping the ball a little higher in the strike zone because his fastball can usually overpower the man at the plate. One of the things that makes the game so enjoyable is the different styles of different pitchers. The fan who watches Morris, Terrell, and Frank Tanana has the pleasure of watching three completely different types of pitchers.

Here is Morris on Morris: "I'd have to put myself in the power-pitcher category. I go after you and either you get me or I get you. My fastball is my best pitch. Everything I throw revolves around it. My forkball [some call it a split-finger fastball] has been quite good over the last couple of years, and I throw a few sliders now and then. I threw a change-up early in my career, but after a few years I got inconsistent with it and it hurt me more than it helped because I was getting be-hind hitters. Now I want to throw it again in situations where I can afford to waste a pitch, but want to show the hitter something off-speed."

Morris's "I'll get you or you get me" creed flies on the banners of most power pitchers. Says Petry, who falls into that class, "Do I play cat-and-mouse guessing games with hitters? Not so much. I'd say it's more strength against strength. Take a guy like George Brett, who's probably the best hitter in baseball, or one of them. He's seen me pitch before, and I've seen him hit. I know how to get him out. So if I can throw the pitch I'm supposed to, I should be able to get him out. But if I don't, that's the pitch he hits out of the park, or at least gets a hit."

The fan can only imagine the exhilaration a Petry or Morris feels in going one-on-one against a George Brett or a hitter of his caliber. Morris, who has thrown a no-hitter and won two World Series games, says: "I can honestly say I think the biggest thrill I've ever had was facing Reggie Jackson when he was with the Yankees and the dominant figure in baseball. It was always a challenge and always a thrill for me to get him out. I don't think there's any hitter in the league today that I can compare that feeling to anymore. Maybe it was because I was young and he was a veteran who was the main man."

The fan who watched any of those battles or today watches a power pitcher try to throw a fastball past a home run hitter should not be surprised to learn that it hurts to throw the ball that hard. "I wish you could feel the way I feel right now," Morris said the day after going only three innings in an exhibition game. "It's usually the day after, the night after, when everything is stiff—not only your arms, but your back, your legs. It's quite strenuous. I don't want to complain about it, because I've accepted that as part of my life, but you really do hurt."

Immediately after he pitches, Morris puts an ice pack on his elbow and shoulder for about 20 minutes. Sometimes he is able to sleep the night after he's pitched, and sometimes he can't. "I always sleep with a long-sleeve shirt on during the season because I'll lose the blood in my elbow at times and it just gets cold," he continues. "My whole forearm might feel cold, and I'll wake up and just feel numbness. It's so cold, I want the shirt for heat. A pitcher, at least in the American League (where designated hitters bat instead of the pitcher), can't do anything on offense to help his team. Everything revolves around our pitching arms. We have to take care of that, because that's our livelihood."

Control pitcher Terrell insists his pitching arm suffers no such trauma. He describes his game as follows: "I throw a sinker [sinking fastball], slider, and change-up. Nothing outstanding, but with good control I can get by. My fastball is anywhere from 84 to 88 miles per hour. 88 if the wind is behind me! I don't think speed is that important. If you stay within yourself, don't try to overthrow, you can stay out of trouble. You're trying to get outs, not throw the ball by the hitters. Anybody that throws the way I do has to keep the ball low, get a lot of ground balls. I'm not gonna strike a lot of people out, and if they're hitting the ball in the air I'm gonna be in trouble."

Muffett agrees that speed is not essential. "Speed is an asset in any game you play, no doubt about it," he says. "But a guy can throw a ball 78 miles an hour and be as effective as a guy who throws it 100 miles per hour. It's all in the movement of the ball. Look at a guy like Frank Tanana."

A good suggestion. The veteran Tanana who has seen his fastball, once one of the tops in the game, grounded because of damage to his wing, has survived quite admirably by learning how to move the ball every which way. Relying on his brain as much as his arm, he falls into the category of "finesse pitcher." A bit of his background before he takes us on a tour of the ins and outs of pitching in and out. When he broke into the major leagues with the California Angels at age 20 in 1973, he was indeed a power pitcher à la Morris. By 1975 he was the American League's top strikeout pitcher, and between '75 and '78 he won 68 games while losing only 40. In 1976 his ERA was a very low 2.44, and in 1977 it was a league-leading 2.54. Then he developed arm trouble. For the next several years he had his ups and downs, but upon being traded to Detroit, his hometown, he experienced a renaissance.

Here is how Tanana describes his baseball life: "At the beginning of my career, I was a power pitcher with control. I was just blessed with the physical tools. I had a real good arm, and I had the long strides. I really used my legs. [The legs are very important. A pitcher is only as strong as his legs, says Muffett.] I had a fastball with speed in the mid 90s, curveball, change-up, and could change speeds on the breaking ball. Control was never a problem. I was confident that I could throw any pitch at any time. Because with my delivery I threw across my body, my fastball would tail back against right-handed hitters and I'd get a lot of inside-corner strikes. Guys would jump back because of the velocity.

"In your youth you don't have to think that much; you let your ability take over more or less. It was nice to be able to rear back and challenge guys, but there wasn't any fear, because you knew you probably had more stuff than they could handle."

Then in 1977, Tanana hurt his elbow. And in 1978, because he was favoring the elbow, his shoulder began to bother him. Although he won 18 games that season, the shoulder hurt all year long and he didn't have his good fastball. "I survived by spotting the fastball and moving the ball around," he says. "I knew then I couldn't challenge people as I once did. I didn't have the stuff."

In 1979 Tanana's arm was so bad that he was unable to pitch and he went on the disabled list. "I told myself I wasn't going to try to get back to where I'd been, that my days of being a power pitcher were over. This was the second major arm injury I'd had—1971 was the other—so I didn't want to tempt fate. There was no telling how many more pitches I had left in the arm." Tanana insists he didn't have any fears about making the transition. He knew he had managed to win 18 games in 1978 without throwing hard and he took heart from the success of such pitchers as Scott McGregor and Tommy John, who relied on guile rather than speed.

Knowing that his fastball was no longer the sort that would inspire scouts to cock their radar guns and say, "Go ahead, make my day," Tanana became more cerebral, less physical. "When you lose that real good fastball," he says, "you have to rely a lot more on your brain, setting up hitters, really moving the ball around, rather than being 2-0 or 3-1 in the count and saying, 'Okay, here comes the fastball. Chances are you can't hit it anyway.' Whereas now if they're sitting expecting the fastball, if I throw it and don't make the pitch, they're gonna hit it hard. Concentration is a must. A guy who doesn't throw hard can't afford to make mistakes out there with that stuff. Right now a good fastball for me might be in the low 80s and the change-up might be 70 miles an hour, maybe 65. But you've still gotta move the hitters around, move them off the plate the best you can. You gotta bust them inside. Yes, even without the good fastball you still have to pitch inside. That keeps them honest. Actually, I wish I'd used my brain early in my career like I'm using it now. I had some good years, but I believe they could have been even better if I'd done more thinking."

While fans look for strikeouts, experienced pitchers look for outs, unless a particular situation calls for the strikeout. Example: Say there is a runner on third base with none out in the later innings of a close game. A ball hit into play may score the runner, so a strikeout is desirable. Says Tanana, "One big difference now is that I'd just as soon get a hitter out with one pitch, whereas before, the strikeout was the big thing and it would take four or five pitches." In his youth Tanana might throw 150 or 160 pitches in a game, where now 100 to 110 is more likely. This obviously saves wear and tear on the arm.

Pitchers in Tanana's boat are always looking for new pitches, and in recent years he has developed several in an effort to keep hitters off balance. "I taught myself the forkball in 1983, and I've also developed a split-fingered sinker-screwball to move away from a right-handed hitter and a little cutter to move in on righties," Tanana says.

Using one's brain on the mound includes setting up hitters—one of the more interesting aspects of pitching. Tanana explains: "The best way I can set a hitter up is by throwing a pitch he's not expecting. So I may go outside with a guy for his first three at bats when the game isn't on the line and stay out there. And then there may come a time when there's a runner in scoring position, and I'll all of a sudden come inside. Throw him something I haven't even shown him his first three times up. So I've set him up. I've let the situation dictate where I'm going to pitch him." (Turnaround is fair play, however. Some hitters, Richie Allen being a notable example, have been rumored to set up pitchers. These hitters, it is said, intentionally look bad on certain pitches, say the curveball, in the early innings when the game is not on the line, hoping that when the game is on the line the pitcher will think he can retire him once again on that pitch. But surprise! The hitter is prepared for the curve, and in Stone's words, "Look out.")

Believe it or not, some savvy pitchers are not only thinking ahead to how they'll pitch to a particular hitter in the later innings, they're thinking ahead to how they'll pitch him in future games. In *The Art of Pitching*, Seaver explains that when he would get a big lead in a ball game, he might try out certain pitches on a batter that he wouldn't try if the game were close. For example, knowing that a slugger's strength was a high fastball, he might throw the pitch anyway to (1) see if he could get him out with that pitch (in which event he might try to use it in future games) and (2) plant the seed that he might throw it in future games (thus forcing the hitter to add one more variable to all future equations).

Stone did the same thing, and thinks all pitchers should too. Noting that teams in the same division play each other 18 times a season, he reasons that a starter could conceivably face an opposing team six times, a particular opposing batter 24 times. "You can't get him out on the same pitch every time," Stone says. "You better find out what he can and can't hit off you."

Of course, the fact that most teams have changed from a four-man to a five-man starting rotation lessens the possibility that a pitcher and hitter will meet as often as Stone suggests. The use of five regular starting pitchers rather than four is a relatively recent development and is not without its detractors, who suggest that it's hard enough to find four quality starters without trying to find a fifth. Others, Hall of Fame pitching great Don Drysdale among them, don't understand the reasoning, which seems to be that over a long season a pitcher will benefit by resting four days in between starts instead of three days. Drysdale notes that pitchers during his career in the 1950s and 1960s not only managed quite well on three days' rest, they generally pitched more innings per start because the age of the relief specialist had not fully dawned.

Drysdale's and others' protests notwithstanding, the age of the five-man rotation is with us. How does a manager set up his rotation? The Tigers' Anderson explains his system: "I don't rate my pitchers one through five. With the balance I have, I like to make my rotation: righty, lefty, righty, lefty, righty. I don't ever want to enter a series without at least one left-hander starting. You'll never get me in a series where we play two games and I pitch two right-handers. Why? Because New York, Toronto, these are great clubs against right-handers, and I don't want to be caught in a series where they get two of them."

Over the years, Anderson's willingness to give the hook to starting pitchers—righty or lefty—relatively early in a game has earned him the nickname Captain Hook. To those who question his tactics, he says, assume that a manager knows what he's doing. "I've actually had pitchers who are scared of losing after the game gets in the 7th inning," he says. "But how would it look the next day in the newspaper if I said, 'I took him out because he was scared.'"

The emergence in recent years of the relief specialist, and Anderson has two capable ones in 1984 Cy Young-winner Willie Hernandez and Mike Henneman, has taken the Captain Hooks of the game off the hook, in a manner of speaking. Virtually every contending team now has what is called a stopper—a relief pitcher who generally takes the mound in the late innings of games in which his team is either holding a small lead or is tied (only on rare occasions will a stopper enter if his team is behind; that role is filled by another specialist). No discussion of pitching would be complete without a look at the stopper, and no stopper is better qualified to discuss his specialty than the Minnesota Twins' Jeff Reardon.

Nicknamed "The Terminator," Reardon is a large man of 30, who wears a beard, in part to intimidate the opposition. In this, he has been highly successful. While with the Montreal Expos in 1985, he led the major leagues in saves, the statistical category by which relief pitchers' effectiveness is measured. And he was near the top of the list again in 1986, 1987, and 1988. He is also consistently among the leaders in two other categories that fans should be aware of—stranding runners (in one two-year period, he entered games with 92 runners on base and only 12 scored) and the success ratio of saves (he saved over four out of every five games he had the opportunity to save).

On the day he spoke to me in 1986 about his craft, Reardon, still with the Expos, entered a game in Wrigley Field against the Cubs with the score tied in the 10th inning. The Cubs had runners on first and second with nobody out. If one of these men scored the game would be over. Reardon is accustomed to coming into such games in the middle of an inning, but now there was an additional variable: he was entering in the middle of an at bat. The Expos' George Riley had been facing the Cubs' Shawn Dunston. Dunston had failed in two sacrifice bunt attempts, and with the bunt no longer a threat (the count was 1-2, and if a batter bunts the ball foul with two strikes, he is out of course, so once this count is reached the bunt is unlikely), manager Bob Rodgers called for his top gun. Reardon promptly retired Dunston on a line drive to center field, then struck out Gary Matthews and Ryne Sandberg on blazing fastballs. Saved from the gallows at the 11th hour, the Expos scored two runs in the 11th inning. Reardon then retired the Cubs, and Montreal had a victory.

During his two innings of work, Reardon threw only two different pitches, the only two pitches he ever throws, the fastball and the curve. Like many stoppers, he was originally a starter—after going 17-4 in the minor leagues in 1978, he was told he'd make it to the big leagues faster as a reliever—and as a starter, he threw the typical fastball, curve, slider, and change-up. What has happened to these last two? "As a reliever you don't have that much time to get a particular pitch going. You want to keep it simple," Reardon explains. "It's not like being a starter, where if a certain pitch isn't working, you can switch to another. In relief if a certain pitch isn't working, you're not going to be in too long. I went with my curve and dropped the slider because my coaches said with my good fastball they'd rather see a slower pitch [for contrast] whereas the slider is a lot harder [faster] than the curve."

How good is his good fastball? It has been clocked in the 89 to 93 miles an hour range. It rises, too, which means Reardon retires more men on popouts and strikeouts than on ground balls. It is Reardon's best pitch, and he says, "Usually I go with my strength, but sometimes I'll get cute, because there are some hitters you just can't throw the fastball past. It seems that those guys are the smaller [lighter] hitters, not the home run hitters. I actually have more trouble with a leadoff-type hitter who's just trying to make contact. I'd rather have someone up there who's trying to go deep. I like that confrontation. Somebody like Jack Clark up with runners on base. I'll get more pumped up with him than, say, a pinch hitter that isn't a home run threat."

Concentrating on only two pitches is only one of several differences between a stopper and a starter. "When I was a starter, I didn't throw on the sidelines very much between starts. I was too stiff, so I just played catch," says Reardon. "But as a reliever you throw every day. It took about a month until my arm got used to that. Then I really got to liking it. Even if I didn't pitch in a game, I would still throw pretty hard every day so I could strengthen my arm."

Reardon thought the mental adjustment of coming to the park prepared to pitch every day would be more difficult than it turned out to be. He found he quickly liked his new role. "If you're a starter and get bombed, you have to wait a whole week to pitch," he explains. "I like being able to help the team every day."

But what about the pressure of coming in when the game is on the line, through none of your own doing? Says Reardon, "You do feel a lot more nervous as a reliever as opposed to a starter. You can have a bad game as a starter and still win. You might be in the clubhouse after giving up five runs and your club might win. But if I have a bad outing, then we're gonna lose the game. That's probably the hardest part of the role—when you blow the game. I take this game real serious, and it bothers me to go out and lose. I'm usually not in a good mood until the next time I do the job. Some guys say, 'It's no big deal. We'll get 'em tomorrow.' But if you think that way, you won't be successful."

When a stopper is not successful, the fans generally let him know it. But during Reardon's early years with the Expos, the fans in the stands even taunted his wife. The harrassment became so troublesome that Reardon considered asking to be traded, but as he improved the boos turned to . . . silence. "The fans in Canada aren't as loud as they are in the States," he says. "What a difference coming to the Twins made. As the 1987 World Series showed America, the cheering in the Metrodome rivals the cheering in any stadium."

Still, if there's any cheering going on in the middle innings, Reardon probably won't hear it. He'll start the game sitting in the dugout so he can watch the opposing hitters, but after the third inning he goes into the clubhouse to stretch and have the assistant trainer work on his shoulder. By the fifth inning, he's out in the bull pen. He usually does not throw unless he gets a call from the dugout, and he can generally get ready in 25 pitches. If a fan were to watch him in the bull pen, he or she would see that Reardon starts out by throwing extra long; he stations the bull pen catcher about 15 feet behind home plate. The fan might also see that Reardon is rarely without a six-pound steel ball given to him by his college coach. "I do exercises with it and hold onto it during the game so that a baseball will feel light and small when I pick it up," Reardon says. "That's why I can get ready so quickly."

Once ready, Reardon, unlike many relief pitchers, keeps throwing. "A lot of guys stand on the mound and just watch after they've thrown their 25 pitches, but I like to keep warm by throwing," he says. "I may throw 60 pitches before I get into the game."

Relief pitchers are said to be the wackiest of ball players. How does Reardon plead? "There are a lot of stories about stoppers being crazy and pulling pranks," he acknowledges, "but I'm not that type of guy. I take it real serious. It's a loose feeling in the bull pen early, but by the middle innings everybody starts thinking about the game, what the situation might be when you come in. The most important thing to think about is getting ahead of the hitter. But how you pitch depends on the circumstances, how many outs. Sometimes you have to go for the strikeout. Other times you just throw strikes and make the hitter hit the ball."

Starting pitchers almost universally state that they cannot gauge how well they will throw in the game based on their pregame bull pen performance. Reardon, however, insists he can often tell how good his stuff is based on his warm-ups. "Sometimes it's frustrating," he says. "You know you've got good stuff but you never get in the game, but when you know you've got your good fastball going and you do get in, that's when you feel you can do no wrong."

Here there is no difference between starting and relieving. Confidence is a must. But Reardon says more than confidence is needed. "I think you have to have a lot of meanness," he says (and it's somewhat hard to believe him for he seems shy, almost gentle off the field). "Everybody hates to lose, but I think a stopper has to hate it more. I keep my distance from other teams. Nowadays, I see a lot of the young pitchers in the league talking to hitters on the opposite team. I don't. I'm not saying you should be real nasty to them, but I don't want them to get to know me. I figure the less they know me the harder it might be for them to hit me."

The loneliness of the stopper. It extends even to his own bailiwick. When a ball player is having trouble hitting, he can talk to the other hitters on his club. Starting pitchers frequently share their common woes. But there is only one stopper on a team. "The stopper is the odd man out," Reardon admits. "There's really nobody to talk to. If a guy goes in before me and has a bad game, I try to talk to him. But if stoppers screw up, people are afraid to talk to us. It usually means the ball game."

Stopper or starter, there are certain things the fan can watch for to determine how well a pitcher is pitching. Many of these are detailed above. As the Cubs' commentator, Steve Stone is, in effect, paid to watch. Here is his free advice to the inquisitive fan:

> I watch the rotation on the breaking pitches—curveball and slider. If it's tight and the ball breaks quickly, I know the pitcher has pretty good stuff that day. If it's lazy and the ball 'rolls,' I know he's got some problems.

Then I watch the catcher, see where he sets up. When a pitcher has his good stuff, he'll throw it within two inches of that glove. If he's missing that glove by a foot, he's gonna have some trouble.

You watch when the pitcher wants to waste a pitch where it goes. You can tell if he's throwing nice and easy or if he's pushing the ball. You watch arm position. If a pitcher who throws over the top suddenly dips to a three-quarters motion [throws more from the side], maybe he has shoulder problems.

Some pitchers give clues when they're struggling. They take a lot more time. Actually, they should be doing just the opposite, because when you're not quite as good, you want your fielders to field better behind you. If you throw more quickly, your fielders will stay on their toes and field better. Slowing down defeats the whole purpose.

Early last season, I spoke with the Yankees' star hitter Don Mattingly about a pitch he happened to strike out on. I had watched this at bat on television, and the announcer had confidently called it a "big, slow curve." But Mattingly insisted it was a fastball.

If you're like I am, you have a hard time figuring out whether a pitch is a fastball, curve, slider, or change-up even when watching it with the wonderful view afforded by a camera over the pitcher's or catcher's shoulder. And it's even more difficult from most vantage points at the ball park.

Steve Stone says not to worry. He admits that many announcers call pitches wrong—it's their radio orientation, he hypothesizes. On radio, you can make up anything you want—but Stone says it doesn't really matter. "The only time you really care what a pitch was is if the guy hits it out of the park," he says. Asked to sum up what different pitches look like, Stone says, "How can I sum up 20 years of experience? Basically, a fastball is faster, a curve breaks down, a slider breaks across, and a straight change-up is slower than everything else."

These and other pitches behave differently from one another because of the way the ball is gripped with respect to the seams, which finger or fingers the pitcher applies pressure with, and the point at which the ball is released.

Within each "species" of pitch there are sub-species. For example, there is a rising fastball, a sinking fastball (or sinker), and now, the split-finger fastball. As its name implies, the **rising fastball**, thrown by power pitchers like Gooden and Reardon, rises as it approaches the plate. It is generally gripped across two of the wide seams of the baseball. This allows all four seams to turn, and that actually makes the ball seem smaller to the batter. (Pitches held across the seams gain rotation and therefore speed. Balls held outside the seams rotate more slowly and are thus less wind resistant. The **knuckleball** scarcely rotates at all, and is therefore subject to all the elements as it heads toward home.) For the rising fastball, many pitchers apply pressure with the middle finger and release it (if they are right-handed) from the equivalent of the 10 o'clock position.

As its name implies, the **sinker** sinks. It is thrown consistently by control pitchers like Terrell and by power pitchers when they want a batter to hit a ground ball, say because they need a double play. The aim is to make the batter hit the top half of the ball, not get under it. This pitch is generally held along the narrow seams and pressure is usually applied by the index finger. It, too, is released from the 10 o'clock position. When a right-handed pitcher throws a sinker to a right-handed batter, his goal is to have the hitter make contact on the thin part of the bat. If the batter is a lefty, the pitcher wants him to hit it off the top end of the bat as it sinks down and away. (There is what is called a "sweet spot" on the bat, a middle zone of perhaps eight inches; pitchers try to avoid this whatever the pitch.)

The **split-finger fastball** is now in vogue. Often confused with the **forkball** (which is slower), this pitch starts out briskly toward the plate looking like a regular fastball, slows down, and then, as if it had been rolling on a table, suddenly drops. Christened by some as the "Pitch of the 80s," the split-finger fastball was popularized by Roger Craig, now the

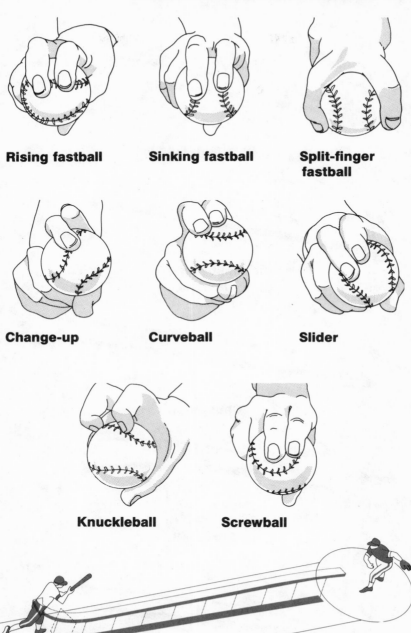

Rising fastball   **Sinking fastball**   **Split-finger fastball**

Change-up   **Curveball**   **Slider**

Knuckleball   **Screwball**

Rising fastball

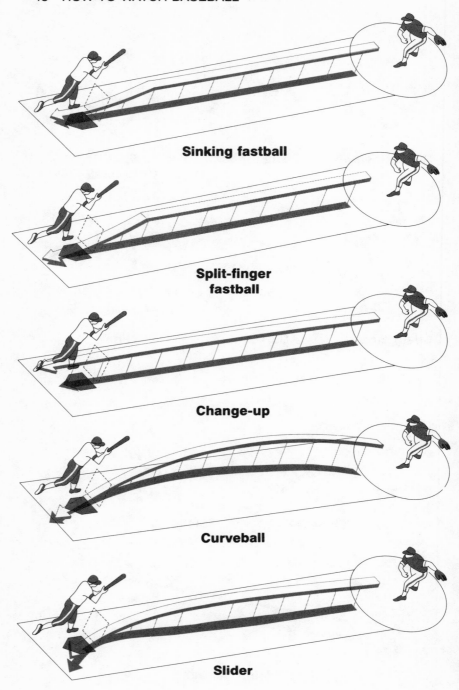

Sinking fastball

Split-finger fastball

Change-up

Curveball

Slider

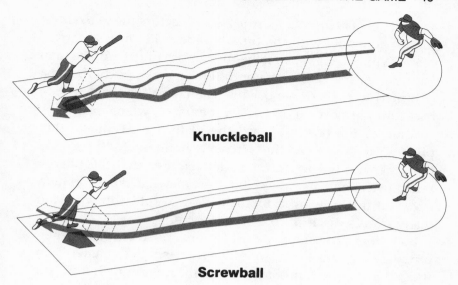

Knuckleball

Screwball

manager of the San Francisco Giants, when he was the Tigers' pitching coach. The pitch is generally thrown with exactly the same motion and arm speed as a fastball, but the grip is different. The fingers are parallel rather than across the seams and are held far apart instead of close together. This is what causes the drop.

The **curve** and the **slider** fall under the heading of "breaking pitches." As most pitchers rely primarily on the fastball, the breaking pitch is thrown to create the impression that a fastball is indeed coming. Then, when it breaks, the batter, who has been expecting a harder pitch up higher, should be confused. A pitcher's curveball may be as much as 10 miles per hour slower than his fastball and when thrown properly will break downward when it is somewhere between 10 to 20 feet from the batter. The slider doesn't break as much as a curve, and it breaks across the plate more than down, but it is equally confounding because it looks like a fastball and doesn't break at all until it is less than 10 feet from the batter. Thrown by a right-hander, these pitches will move down and away from right-handed hitters and down and in on left-handed hitters. (The **screwball** does the reverse.)

The curve is gripped, like the fastball, across the two widest seams, generally with the thumb on the side near a narrow seam. With the curve, a pitcher uses more finger surface than with the fastball. Other major differences: the pitcher's wrist is turned to the side, and while the fastball is thrown with backspin, the curve is thrown with topspin, which means the rotation of the ball is toward the plate. Unlike most other pitches, which leave the pitcher's hand with the simple movement of the wrist, the slider requires that the pitcher pull down slightly with his elbow—somewhat like the motion involved in throwing a football. As a result, throwing too many sliders can lead to elbow trouble.

Both the curve and the slider are most effective when thrown low in the strike zone. If a right-handed pitcher is on the mound he will probably try to throw the pitch low and away to a right-handed hitter, but it can also be effective high and inside to a left-handed hitter. If either the curve or the slider "hang" in the strike zone, the pitcher is in trouble. The ball, without the speed or movement of the fastball, will be sitting high in the strike zone, almost as if on a tee waiting for the batter to hit it. A lot of home runs are hit on bad sliders.

A pitcher with a good **change-up** will throw it with the same motion, hand position, arm speed, and angle of delivery as the fastball. The crucial difference is in the grip and pressure points, which are altered to reduce the velocity of the pitch. The change-up is used to throw the batter's timing off. It looks like the fastball as it approaches the plate and the pitcher's deceptive motion makes the batter think "fastball." But this is a case of mistaken identity. The change-up takes a lot longer to get to the plate. So now the hitter must worry that if he is set for a fastball he will instead get a change-up and swing far too early. In addition, properly spotted the change-up makes the fastball look that much faster.

3
HITTING: NO PLACE TO HIDE

Hidden far behind the playing field, deep below the center field walls, there sits in Boston's Fenway Park a dank rectangle of a room described, charitably, by the Red Sox's right fielder Dwight Evans as "a dungeon." At 4 P.M. every day when the Red Sox are playing at home, Evans and teammate Rich Gedman leave the safe haven of the club-house, cross the ball park's rich, green grass, then bid good bye to the sun and, one at a time, enter this space.

Waiting for the players is Walt Hriniak, the Red Sox coach and batting instructor. Hriniak is a stolid New Englander whose voice betrays emotion only when talking about his two great loves, his daughter Jill and baseball. He is rheumy-eyed and ruddy cheeked, his blond hair is atangle under his cap, and he almost always is carrying a large blue duffel bag over his shoulder. He looks like a sailor who has just reached port after crossing the stormy Atlantic in a small craft.

Hriniak, who left the Red Sox after the 1988 season, puts down the bag and takes a seat on a folding chair set a few feet behind a screen that is perhaps seven feet high and five feet wide. He opens the bag, and with a pair of hands that verify that he was a catcher for 13 years, pulls out several baseballs. The barrel-chested Gedman, the Red Sox's catcher, moves to a plate only a few yards from his coach, then, his bat held out in front of him as if it were a divining rod, he searches for the perfect stance. Or trance—so intense is his concentration as he makes sure his feet, hands, and head are properly positioned.

Finally comfortable, Gedman nods to Hriniak, who from behind the screen gently underhands the ball. Crack! Gedman drives the ball into the webbing. Crack! Another solid hit. Swoosh! A weak popup that hits the dungeon's low roof. "Keep your head down," says Hriniak, who tosses balls and suggestions for 15 minutes, then repeats the procedure with Evans.

The scene seems familiar. And so it is. How many fathers and mothers, having taken to the backyard to toss the ball underhanded to sons and daughters just learning how to hit, have sung the anthem: "Keep your eye on the ball."

But this is the major leagues. Gedman and Evans are both premiere hitters who have made the All Star team. What are these proven players doing swinging at underhanded pitching delivered from such close range?

"I've asked the greatest players in every sport, and they agree that if you had to pick the hardest thing to do in any game, it's hit the baseball," says Ted Williams, the Red Sox legend and one of the game's greatest hitters. "You've got so many elements going on there. You have to have such quick hand-eye coordination. You've got curveballs, fastballs, sliders, different deliveries, different angles that the ball comes to the plate. And you're trying to hit a round ball with a round bat."

Hriniak agrees: "Hitting is an endurance contest. It's so deep that it's mind-boggling. You have to deal with so many things. The pitcher. Failure. Forty thousand people booing. Exposure. If I ever write a book about hitting, I'll call it 'No Place to Hide.' A stadium full of people. One million more watching you on television. Nine against one in the field. The odds are completely against you. You play basketball and somebody can throw you a good pass. Same thing in hockey. In football, someone can block for you. Hitting, there's no one to turn to, no place to hide. You strive for perfection, but perfection is impossible, so you're happy if you succeed on three out of every 10 chances."

The deck was not always so stacked against the hitter. Until 1883, pitchers actually had to deliver the ball underhanded. Until 1887, the man at the plate had the right to demand either a high pitch or a low pitch from the man on the mound. And not until 1888 was the "three strikes and you're out" rule adopted.

But the game has evolved so that the odds in the battle between pitcher and hitter clearly favor the man who controls the ball and initiates the action. In 1941, his best season—the best season any batter has had in well over half a century—Williams batted .406. This means he still made six outs for every four hits he got. Today a team that bats .265 for a season is doing quite well.

Yet, in recent years a new generation of first-rate hitters has emerged. Why? Some observers say it is because athletes are simply physically stronger and better conditioned than in the past. Others argue that the advent of artificial turf has led to more hits because balls bounce or scoot through a synthetic infield faster than through a grass one (the St. Louis Cardinals' Willie McGee is a prime example of a player who takes advantage of such a surface). One player even has gone so far as to suggest that politics may be the reason. His farfetched theory: Baseballs are manufactured in Haiti. After "Baby Doc" Duvalier removed himself from power, the workers in that nation were happier and became more productive. They therefore wound the baseballs tighter, making them more "alive," easier to hit.

Anatomy, technology, and politics notwithstanding, the

pitcher still maintains the advantage. This is not surprising, as he is only 60 feet 6 inches from home plate, and either is throwing a ball 90 miles an hour that rises or falls or moves in or out, or is throwing a ball that looks as if it might be traveling at that speed but all of a sudden, as if influenced by some distant ground control, seems to slow down or change trajectory so that it curves or slides away from the well-planned arc of the swinging bat.

The poor batter must immediately pick up the ball—a deadly object—when it leaves the pitcher's hand, decide *if* he is going to swing, then, if the answer is yes, must decide *how and where* to swing. Then, he must execute the swing. All this in less than a second and a half, for that is all it takes a pitch to reach the plate. Perhaps he will be fortunate enough to make contact. But making contact is hardly enough. He must hit the ball so that it will not be caught. A tall order.

Thus the daily journey to the dungeon by perfectionists Gedman, Evans, and Buckner and batting practice for all before each game. If there is only a split second at the plate to prepare for the delivered pitch, there is much that can be done before going to the plate. The more methodical, rhythmic the hitter can be—and this can be achieved through practice—the more he will be able to concentrate exclusively on meeting the ball when the game begins.

Come out early to the park and watch batting practice. Most teams divide their hitters into groups of four or five and give each group about 15 minutes to hit. As a group's time runs down, watch how all the players—veterans and .300 hitters included—rush to the plate so that they can get in their final swings. Practice will never make a batter perfect, but the difference between a star .300 hitter and an adequate .260 hitter is only four hits every 100 at bats.

While his hitters would no doubt concur that there is no place to hide once you enter the batter's box, they do not feel quite as alone as Hriniak modestly suggests. Since Hriniak joined the coaching staff in 1977, the Red Sox's hitters have had someone to turn to—a longtime student of the art of putting bat to ball who has become the game's foremost instructor. And, along with Hall of Famer Williams, the perfect guide to explain how to watch hitters.

It should be noted that even before Hriniak arrived in Boston, the Red Sox were never shortchanged at the plate. Fenway Park with its short right field and even more inviting short left field climaxed by the wall known as the Green Monster has always been a hitter's paradise. The history of the Red Sox is a history of batting champions and home run kings. Some of these ball players—Williams and Carl Yastrzemski, for example—would have been superstars wherever they played, but others clearly enjoyed banner years because they played in Fenway.

"The park in which you play makes a tremendous difference," says Ken "Hawk" Harrelson. Harrelson, a power hitter, enjoyed good years at the plate playing in Kansas City's spacious park from 1963 to 1967 and Cleveland's expansive stadium from 1969 to 1971. Sandwiched in between those tours of duty was the year 1968, when he hit 35 home runs and led the major leagues in runs batted in. Where was he? Boston. What happened? "I didn't become a better player overnight," he admits. "A lot of it had to do with the fact that I was playing in Fenway."

Harrelson cites another reason good hitters turn into great ones, if only for a season or two—the lineup in which they are playing. In Kansas City, Harrelson had been the team's principal home run threat, and opposing pitchers, well aware of this, had pitched around him. That is, rather than give him a good pitch to hit, they tempted him with poorer pitches. They were even willing to walk him—and pitchers hate to give up walks—because they knew that those following him in the order were not particularly dangerous. (Today, this happens frequently to George Brett.) In Boston, Harrelson was in the middle of a lineup so potent that pitchers rarely pitched around him, and thus he received better pitches to hit.

There is no place to hide for the pitchers facing the current

Red Sox either. Boston's longtime player, manager, and coach Johnny Pesky thinks that man-for-man this may be the best-hitting team in Red Sox history. In 1985, the team hit a major league-leading .282 and scored 800 runs, tops in the game. Those figures were better than those posted by the Red Sox championship teams of 1967 and 1975.

While it may not be a surprise that today's Red Sox team can hit, it is surprising how the hitting is done. Unlike the Sox of old, the Hriniak-coached hitters rarely try to pull the ball to take advantage of the short left field. They try to hit the ball to all fields, to use the whole park. This is an essential element of the Hriniak philosophy, a philosophy passed down by his mentor, the late Charlie Lau.

Lau, who was the hitting instructor for the Royals, then the Yankees, and then the White Sox—all of whom won titles during his stays—was undeniably the guru of hitting in the 1970s and 80s. He was one of the first coaches to utilize videotape, not only to analyze particular players' strengths and weaknesses but to develop what he called "the absolutes of hitting." (Before the advent of videotape, some instructors used motion pictures. Longtime baseball executive Roland Hemond recalls that the Milwaukee Braves' batting coach Paul Waner employed film in the 1950s. "Trouble was," smiles Hemond, "by the time the film got developed the team was either out of town or the hitter was in such a slump that the pictures weren't always that helpful.")

Lau was so effective that when the White Sox, winners of the 1983 American League West divisional championship, slipped to fifth place the following season, owner Jerry Reinsdorf was absolutely convinced that the drop was due to Lau's absence while he fought an unsuccessful battle against cancer. There are Lau believers throughout baseball, including such stars as the Red Sox's Wade Boggs, the White Sox's Carlton Fisk, the Yankees' Don Mattingly, and the Royals' Brett. Brett, who was not an outstanding hitter in the minor leagues, still credits Lau for much of his good fortune.

So, too, does a man who feels he would have been

marooned in the minor leagues had it not been for Lau—Walt Hriniak. Lau's impact as Hriniak's minor-league manager was so great that Hriniak decided to become a hitting instructor after his playing days ended. Now the foremost disciple of Lau's teachings, Hriniak reverentially recites the philosophy chapter and verse. After hearing it, you should have little difficulty in determining whether the batter you are watching is also an adherent. Here is Lau, according to Hriniak:

- "You have to have a balanced, workable stance. It's like building a house. You have to have a strong foundation to build a second and third tier."
- "There has to be movement in the stance to create a rhythm and a tension-free swing. There has to be movement back before you go forward, just like in anything else in sports where you're projecting an object forward with some kind of force."
- "You shift your weight from the back side to the front side."
- "You get good extension with your arms, good follow-through by releasing the top hand from the bat after you hit the ball."
- "You learn to watch the baseball. And the way to watch the baseball is what we call being able to 'discipline your head,' put your head down on the baseball."
- "Use the whole field. Don't try to hit a home run unless it's absolutely necessary. You get in trouble that way. Try to hit the ball right back at the pitcher."
- "Don't stand too close to the plate."
- "Land with the front toe closed."

Lau was a marginal player batting only .255 and hitting only 16 home runs over an 11-year career that saw him bounce between the big leagues and the minors. Hriniak, despite Lau's tutelage, only had 99 major-league at bats and 25 hits, all singles. Ted Williams batted .344 and hit 521 home runs over his illustrious career, winning seven batting titles, the last one when he was 40 years old. This he accomplished by not using the whole park, but pulling the ball to right field. Indeed, so well known was this predilection that teams would shift their shortstops to the other side of second base in order to defend against him. Williams, who managed at Washington and Texas after retiring and still coaches the Red Sox minor leaguers, finds heretical the teachings of Lau and Hriniak (who, of course, coaches the minor leaguers once they become major leaguers). "The main reason I've gone to batting clinics the last 15 years is to say they're wrong," he told me one morning during spring training in 1986.

He was interrupted by a fan, who asked him to sign a large photograph taken during the 1940s. In the picture, Williams had just hit a home run. "See my head. I'm looking up. See my bat. See my hips," said Williams. "You can't hit for power if you don't open your hips. And you can't hit for power if you're swinging down on the ball the way those guys teach. You have to swing up."

Hriniak's response: "Of all the hitters over the last 35 years to hit for a high average and hit home runs, Ted Williams is the only one who didn't use the whole field." Beyond that, says Hriniak, their differences are not in the mechanics of hitting, but in the semantics. "I don't teach people to swing down. I teach them to start down and finish up. At the moment of contact, you should be level or slightly up." As for the hips? "I teach hips, but I don't use the word *hips*. I use the words *extension* and *high finish*. The hips obviously have to come into the swing. You need a good hip turn, or opening. If you don't get it you're restricted. But as soon as you start teaching, *hips*, you lose the ball. You lose the discipline of concentrating on your head. You get on your heels, and you can't hit. By thinking *high finish* and *let go of the bat*, you get the same results. You're still able to maintain the discipline of your head. The most important thing in hitting is the ability to see the ball as long and as soon as you can. That's why I never say, 'hips, hips, hips.' I say, 'high finish, high finish,' and the hips come into play."

Whatever their differences, real or imagined, with regard to stance and swing, Hriniak and Williams agree that hitting can be taught and that it requires as much mental skill as physical prowess. Says Hriniak, "I don't believe hitters are born. Obviously you have to have a certain amount of talent, but it's the good mechanics, the good absolutes, the desire to practice hard and improve that makes a good hitter. A lot of people say, 'You can either hit or you can't.' I don't believe that. I've seen too many hitters get better in the big leagues."

Adds Williams, "When I was managing, I was able to improve almost all my hitters by working from here up." He points to his head as he talks. "The thinking part of hitting."

The thinking part of hitting. Different pitchers pitch differently to the same batter. One pitcher might feel he'll be more successful relying on the curveball; another may be convinced that the fastball is more likely to trouble the hitter. As the chapter on pitching indicates, pitchers try to outfox batters from pitch to pitch, from at bat to at bat, from game to game. They change speeds; they change the location—inside, outside, up, down. "Sometimes the pitcher will throw you a nice pitch to hit; then the next time you're up he won't throw you anything. That's the game, you know," philosophizes the California Angels' fielder Tony Armas.

But patterns also emerge. "You have to know what to look for in certain situations," says Hriniak. "Unfortunately a lot of hitters get themselves out by not thinking. For instance, if you charted a baseball game, you'd see that some right-handed pitchers in our league throw the ball from the middle of the plate to the outside of the plate about 90 percent of the time when they're facing right-handed batters. By design. Yet some hitters will look for that one pitch inside that never seems to come, instead of preparing to hit the ball from the middle of the plate out into centerfield or right field. They go up there trying to pull the ball to left, but the pitcher isn't going to let them pull."

Adds Mike Easler, a .300 hitter in three of his first seven years, "Pitchers know your strengths and weaknesses, and they'll keep going to your weakness until you prove them wrong. Then they'll move on to something else. It's a cat-and-mouse game. That's what makes baseball so exciting."

Read the postgame interview with the man who batted in the winning run, and you'll often see that he says, "I was looking for a fastball in that situation." Or "I just figured he'd throw me a breaking pitch, and he did." Most hitters—Boston's potent Jim Rice is a notable exception—will often try to guess that a particular pitch is coming. Explains Easler, "It's just a feeling that you have out there. It's just a God-given feeling. You know what the pitcher's 'out' pitch is. You know the catcher—how he calls a game with nobody on base or a runner on third with nobody out. It's just a feeling. And when you're going good that feeling is beautiful."

The Red Sox's Wade Boggs, who batted .366 in 1988, goes one step further. "I try to work the count so that I feel I'm gonna get the pitch I want and then go from there."

Working the count so that you can force the pitcher to throw the pitch you want requires a discipline that few hitters possess. Some players—the Los Angeles Dodgers' Mickey Hatcher is a good example—care little for the count or situation. They swing at anything close to the strike zone. Not so Boggs. "I've never seen a guy with the discipline that Wade has," says former teammate Easler. "Being patient. Waiting for the right pitch. Ted Williams talks about zones. If you swing at pitches in one zone, you'll end up hitting .250. If you're more disciplined, you'll only swing at pitches in the .300 zone. You have to know what your zone is and be consistent. Wade is perfect; he knows his zone."

Boggs has the perfect attitude for approaching hitting. He enters what he describes as a "cocoon" every day he is playing so that he can eliminate all distractions. "Hitting requires a tremendous amount of discipline and concentration," he says. He and Hriniak meet daily. "We'll talk for about 30 minutes about who's pitching. It's sort of like getting a game plan for the day."

Scouting reports can clue hitters to particular pitchers' tendencies, and some players keep books on pitchers, noting what was thrown when so that they can pick up patterns. Boggs however, does not take pen to paper. "It's all up in my head," he says. "I don't write anything down."

Neither does Hriniak. "I just take it game to game," he says. "Pitchers might not have their good curveball and you have to pick that up from the way the game is going. I'll follow the pitcher, see how he's attacking certain hitters and certain situations. He might throw the fastball with nobody on or nobody in scoring position, but every time a man gets in scoring position, this particular pitcher for some reason has decided he won't get beat on his fastball, that he's only gonna give you a chance to beat him by throwing the curve. That trend will emerge."

It takes Hriniak one trip through the lineup before he can really spot these trends. Once onto something he will share it with any interested party on the bench. "Some guys will lean on me more than others," he says. "I'm there for their health. If I feel I should say something I will. But I don't try to force myself on anybody."

Players share their findings with each other, too. The astute fan might notice that sometimes a batter who has just struck out will pause on his way back to the dugout to speak to the man in the on-deck circle. Similarly, once a batter, successful or not, gets back to the bench, his teammates may approach him. Says Gedman, "You ask each other how the pitcher's throwing. What's his fastball doing? What about his slider—is it going down or across?"

Gedman is selective in his questioning. "I try not to ask about speed, because speed isn't the same to everybody. You're looking at it through somebody else's eyes. I'm more interested in knowing where the pitcher is trying to get the ball with certain hitters."

Gedman studies the pitcher himself not only while on the bench but in the on-deck circle as well (you can tell a good deal about a player's intensity by watching him in the on-deck circle). "When I'm in the on-deck circle, I'm trying to time the pitcher, get my timing down in terms of getting out at the ball.

I'm acting as if I'm up at the plate already. I'm not so concerned about the pitch as I am with release points and getting my timing down for my swing."

The release point, as the name suggests, is the point at which the pitcher releases the ball. To decipher a pitch and time his swing, the batter must be able to pick the ball up as soon after it is released as possible. How does a batter do this and how can a fan do it? "A lot of pitchers release the fastball different from the way they release a breaking ball. You have to see this just at that instant when the pitcher is right on top and releases the ball right out of his hand. Then you can tell," says the Oakland A's powerful designated hitter Don Baylor. Some hitters claim they can tell what a pitch is going to be by the way the stitching on the ball spins, but "It's not the spin, it's the direction that the ball takes, if it moves away from you or into you," says Baylor. "As far as seeing the breaking ball, you know as a right-handed hitter it's going to start to your left and move to your right."

When talking about spotting trends, Hriniak sounds curiously like those assistant football coaches who sit high above the playing field, detect patterns, and phone their observations down to the men on the sidelines. A similarity exists, too, in the use of videotape. Hriniak spends countless hours during the off-season and after games viewing replays of his batters. Today, virtually every major-league clubhouse has a VCR, and many players watch themselves at the park before a game or even at home. Says Easler, "You take tapes home after the season and watch where your hands are, how your head is placed on the ball. You can even get a feeling for how each team pitches you."

While knowing what the pitcher may throw is important, it is equally important to feel comfortable and confident at the plate. "If you go out there feeling like you're gonna hit the ball right at somebody or that no matter what happens you're not gonna get a hit, you're beat," says Red Sox second baseman Marty Barrett.

Adds Buckner, "Everybody has a certain amount of physical ability. Now it's up to you to prepare yourself for the game and be confident. Some guys don't perform up to their abilities because they worry about what happened in the past and what's going to happen in the future."

As confident as they may seem through their public personas, few players can avoid such periods of self-doubt over the course of the season. "You play 162 games a year," says Rice. "Somewhere down the line, you have to break down."

Left-handed batters traditionally hit better against right-handed pitchers, and right-handed batters have an easier time with lefties. Thus, when the right-handed-hitting Rice is going poorly, he comes to the park hoping that he will be facing a left-handed pitcher. "At least you can pick the ball up from the delivery a little sooner," he says. Also, "You love to see someone that you know you can hit or at least some guy that you can see the ball well off of."

And whom does Rice prefer to see pitching when he has his confidence and is hitting well? "When you're swinging the bat well, you don't care," he says, smiling.

When a batter is swinging well, "the feeling is like the difference between night and day," says Easler. "When you're not going well the ball looks very, very small. Everything is on the outside corner, inside corner of the plate. Nothing is down the middle. But when you're going good, the ball looks like it's in slow motion."

Adds Baylor, "When things are right, it seems that every pitch is just sitting there on a tee. You're blocking out the fans. You're blocking out everything else. The ball is just right there."

Many batters describe this odd sensation, and Buckner, converted to the Lau-Hriniak school after coming to the Red Sox from the Cubs 13 seasons into a successful career, thinks he has an explanation. "When you're hitting well, the ball doesn't look as fast because your approach at the ball is good.

You're keeping your head down and you're keeping it still throughout the swing. When you're moving your head alot, the ball looks like it's going a lot faster."

Critics of Lau and Hriniak argue that keeping the head down and following the other absolutes may translate into singles but that it's impossible to hit for power that way. Nonsense, replies Hriniak, who points to the success of, among others, Evans, Armas (who is no longer with the Red Sox) and Gedman.

Looking almost knock-kneed, standing almost tiptoed in the batter's box, Evans, says Hriniak, "has the classic Charlie Lau stance." ("Watching Evans almost makes me want to vomit," says Williams.) He came to Hriniak for help while struggling at the plate in 1980 and has hit for not only better average but more power as well. In the strike-shortened 1981 season, he tied for the American League lead in home runs.

Armas came to Boston from the Oakland Athletics in 1983. Already a bona fide slugger, he hit 36 home runs his first year with Boston. But he batted only .218. "We didn't think that was good enough," says Hriniak, who worked with him not only on his mechanics (to try and level out an exaggerated uppercut swing), but also on his approach to the game (to try to get him to stop trying to pull everything and to use the whole field). Hriniak's biggest obstacle was persuading a wary Armas that the long ball would still come if he followed this new regimen. If the coach wasn't persuasive enough, the results of the experiment were. Armas raised his average 50 points to a respectable .268, and he actually hit for more power, leading the league with 43 home runs and 123 runs batted in.

The hardworking, left-handed-hitting Gedman's story is equally dramatic:

Gedman: "A few years ago, I felt I needed a change. I thought, 'Jeez, I feel like I'm as good as I'm gonna get. There's gotta be something more to it, because I know I'm a better player than I'm showing.' I couldn't pull the ball at all. I was a flat-footed hitter. I hit more on my heels. Everything was a force or a grunt, sort of like a bull in a china shop. There was no rhythm. Everything was my power against the pitcher's power, and anytime I got a breaking ball to hit, I'd be so off balance that I never had a chance. So I went to Walt."

Hriniak: "When I first saw Richie, he stood way off the plate with an extremely closed stance and hit everything to left field. If the ball was thrown from the middle of the plate out, he could hammer it. But if the ball was thrown inside, he'd just try to yank it out of there with his top hand. He just couldn't hit the ball inside."

Gedman: "Walt totally reconstructed my swing. He taught me to relax, to get the full advantage of my weight shift from going back to going forward, but not only that, to have an extension. Not cutting off your swing, but giving it a chance to survive."

Hriniak: "He made the adjustment with his feet himself after spending some time in winter ball; he jumped up on top of the plate with an open stance. What I taught him was the importance of being able to hit the ball with your front arm extended instead of trying to pull the ball with your top hand. I tried to show him the importance of trying to get back into your stance and to be able to lead to the baseball with the bottom half first. I explained the importance of being able to maintain the discipline of the head, of putting your head down on the baseball and leaving it there even longer than you think is necessary. I tried to show him the importance of starting down at the baseball and then going up. In my opinion, there's no such thing as a level swing. To get level or slightly up at the ball at the moment of contact, you must start down. If you start up, the swing has a tremendous loop in it and you're slowing down your bat."

Gedman: "The aim wasn't to hit more home runs—if the home runs came, fine—it was just to be a better hitter. Just give myself a better chance. I went from being able to hit the ball hard once in a while to being able to hit it consistently hard. I could hit more pitchers than before, hit breaking balls, change-ups. I could hit lefties and righties. Walt said the home runs would come in time. First you have to do these things, then everything will fall in place."

In time Gedman's home run production improved dramatically. Playing in half the Red Sox's games in 1982 and 1983, he hit only six home runs in about 500 at bats. In 1984 and 1985, he hit a total of 42 home runs in less than 950 trips to the plate.

Just as pitchers don't always try to throw strikes, batters—even those not in Hriniak's camp—don't always try to hit home runs. Says Rice, who has led the American League in home runs three times: "Normally you try to go to the plate and make solid contact, but sometimes you go up there looking for the home run. It's usually if the game is a blowout where you're down several runs or if you're six or seven runs up, it's the 7th inning, and you already have three hits." Some power hitters may also try if the game is on the line in the late innings, particularly with two out and nobody on base.

Rice, who consults periodically with Hriniak but swings to the beat of his own drummer, does not change his stance when he is going for the fences. "You try to be a little more selective with pitches, try to pick up the ball a little sooner, try to get the head of the bat out so you're quicker with the bat," he says.

Can a fan tell if a Hriniak believer is trying to hit a home run? Not from his stance or swing, but there may be another clue. "The way to hit a home run is not to change your mechanics," says Hriniak. "It's pitch selection and your position in the batter's box. To try to hit a home run, you have to try and pull. When you try and pull, you move closer to the plate, but you don't change anything else. You look for the ball from the middle of the plate in; you hit the ball when it's a little bit further out in front of the plate to try and pull it, but that's it."

Is there a part of the bat where Hriniak wants his players to hit the ball? He laughs. "Yeah. That's what we call the sweet spot. It's about three or four inches from the top end of the bat."

Can he tell when someone hits a ball on the sweet spot? "No." He pauses, then laughs. "Well, you can tell by where the ball goes."

Most fans, of course, watch exactly that—where the ball goes. Hriniak doesn't, and he advises that the fan who periodically wants to analyze a hitter skip the familiar maxim and not keep his or her eyes on the ball. Here is how Hriniak watches a hitter:

"I begin watching way before the ball is thrown. I watch his stance, watch how he's moving in the batter's box. Good hitters have good rhythm, and they maintain that rhythm all the time. Just like a golfer who is sitting over a golf ball, they have the same movements on the first hole as they do on the 72nd hole on the fourth day of the tournament. It sets the tempo for them. That's very important in hitting. Watch and you'll see each player has his own tempo.

"I never watch the ball after it hits the bat. All good hitters, even after they hit the ball, maintain good balance. There are exceptions once in a while, but usually, they don't fall off the ball. I watch the batter hit and then make sure where the bat finishes, if there's good follow-through, and more important than that, how was the discipline of the head? The head happens so fast that if you're not really watching and somebody asks you: 'Where was his head? Up? Down?' You don't know unless you're watching.

"I've heard people say that you can tell that a batter got a good swing if he fouls the ball straight back. I suppose that if the batter had a good, tension-free, fluid extended swing and his head was good, yeah, he'd hit the ball straight back. But you better not foul too many back. I hear it all the time, 'Oh, I just missed it. I just missed it.' Well, how many times can you just miss it?"

And how does Williams watch?

"The first thing you look for is overall quickness and the ability to get the bat on the ball. Now, if a guy's got a quick swing and getting the ball on the bat, he's seeing the ball right. Then you look where he's swinging—under or over? After you play five or six years, you know you have to correct swings against certain types of pitchers. There are some pitchers that make the ball look like it rides. Actually it doesn't ride that much, but it stays straight a little longer and you swing at it and it's over your bat all the time. Well, watch a good hitter. After one swing like that, he says, 'This guy's a little quicker than he looks. I gotta be quicker.'

"I say, 'Gee the hitter didn't open up his hips,' or 'He swung at a bad ball,' or 'He tried to pull that pitch and he hadn't even seen a pitch.' I'll watch a pitcher and see his style and say, 'Gee, you gotta have a fastball here.' And then he throws it, and the hitter is late swinging. That immediately tells me that I know what the pitcher's doing, but the hitter ain't thinking what's going on. I'm still playing that game between the hitter and the pitcher."

A Day At the Office

Don Mattingly, the New York Yankees' first baseman, is cut from the same cloth as the legendary Williams in that he hits for both average and power. In 1984, the first season in which he played in more than 95 games, Mattingly led the American League in batting with a .343 average, hit 23 home runs, and batted in 110 runs. In 1985, his average "slipped" to .324, but he hit 35 home runs and drove in 145 runs, tops in the major leagues. He was named the American League's Most Valuable Player. He had fine years at the plate in '86, '87, and '88 as well.

When the Yankees journeyed to Chicago for a three-game series over the 4th of July weekend in 1986, Mattingly was batting over .340 with 13 home runs and 57 r.b.i.'s. The White Sox beat the Yanks 2-1 on July 4. Mattingly, who felt he had not been swinging well in earlier days, was hitless and became so frustrated after one at bat that he went down to the runway under the dugout and threw his helmet.

The next day he was back on track, pounding a double and a triple in five at bats as the Yankees won 8-0. The morning after this game he talked to me about his trips to the plate and in so doing revealed that even the best hitters in the game can feel lost in the batter's box.

JULY 5, 1986

The left-handed-hitting Mattingly is batting second in the lineup, behind Claudell Washington. Joe Cowley, a 6'5" right-hander, who came to the White Sox from the Yankees, is on the mound. In an earlier game this season, he set an American League record by striking out the first seven men he faced. Today he starts by striking out Washington on a pitch on the outside edge of the plate. Mattingly watched Cowley for two seasons in New York. He knows what to expect—"I know that he basically pitches away," he says—but does not go up to the plate looking for a particular pitch. Cowley's first pitch is away, a called strike on the outside corner of the plate. The next pitch is inside, and Mattingly fouls it off. Cowley appears to double pump on the next pitch. Mattingly is out in front of the ball; he misses, strikes out. "The double pump had nothing to do with me missing," says the hitter. "He just got me on a slow curve."

Mattingly's second at bat comes in the third inning. There is one out and a runner on second base. The Yankees lead 2-0. Having faced Cowley once and struck out, does Mattingly make any adjustments? No. "I didn't make any adjustments based on the way he pitched me. I was just trying to find my swing there. It was kind of lost. I'd had bad swings the day before and the day before that, too. And I had no idea what I was doing up there." (Even the best have their off-days, it seems.)

The count goes to 2-0. "Here, I'm looking for a fastball to hit. I want to swing at a strike [not at a pitch out of the strike zone] and I'm looking to go to left field with the ball [keeping in mind that Cowley is pitching him away]." Mattingly gets his pitch and hits it to left. But it is a routine fly ball easily handled by the Sox's Reid Nichols. "I didn't feel that I hit it very well," says Mattingly.

At bat number three comes with two out and nobody on in the fifth inning. The Yanks now lead 5-0. Cowley is no longer pitching, having been replaced by left-handed rookie Joel McKeon. "You face a lefty a little differently," says Mattingly, "but at the time my big concern is just trying to see the ball and hit it. I still don't know what I'm doing." He looks confused on the first pitch and is unable to check his swing. Strike one. But he makes good contact with McKeon's next offering (a pitch in the strike zone), driving it deep over center fielder John Cangelosi's head for a triple. "I saw it all right, but probably if it had been a ball I'd have swung at it, too. Because I've been swinging at everything they throw up there the last few days," he says. "Fortunately it was in the strike zone and I did hit it pretty well."

When Mattingly comes to the plate in the eighth inning, he faces his third pitcher of the day, right-handed veteran Gene Nelson. Nelson has been struggling lately, and in this inning Washington hit his first pitch, a fastball, for a home run. Mattingly's plan of attack? "I was gonna try and do the same thing [try to hit a fastball over the fence], but he gave me a slider and I pulled it foul. Again, I'm still swinging at everything." He swings at the next two pitches as well, fouling off one, then hitting a double.

He gets his fifth and final chance of the day in the ninth inning, and grounds out on a 1-1 pitch. In discussing this final at bat, he becomes a bit impatient. "You see, you do the same thing every time up," he explains. "You just look for the ball." But isn't it more scientific than that? "You want to be scientific in batting practice. When you get in the game you don't think anymore. You just see the ball and try and hit it hard."

It's as simple and as difficult as that.

4
DEFENSE:
THE BALLET NO
ONE WATCHES

Quickly now, how many ball players can you name who were elected to the Hall of Fame primarily because of defense? Pee Wee Reese, the Dodgers' spunky shortstop in the 1950s. And Brooks Robinson, the Orioles' classy third baseman. But try to name another.

Now name an active player picked for the All-Star team in recent years in either league because of his glovework. Ozzie Smith, the St. Louis Cardinals' graceful shortstop, is one. Can you think of anybody else?

"Baseball," says Smith, "has always been a more offense-oriented game, but it's really the defense that gets your club in the position to win. I guess it dates back to the days of Babe Ruth. Fans just enjoy seeing the ball go over the fence. But I don't care how good an offensive club you are, without a good defense behind you, things are going to catch up to you at some point during the season."

Smith's former teammate, pitcher John Tudor, is the first to agree. Toiling five years on mediocre defensive clubs in

Boston and Pittsburgh, Tudor compiled a less than earthshaking record of 51 wins and 43 losses. Traded to the Cardinals before the 1985 season, he suddenly blossomed. His statistics: a 21-8 record, 1.93 earned run average, and 10 shutouts.

What accounted for the turnaround? Tudor claims that mechanically he was basically the same pitcher he had always been, but that playing in Busch Stadium with the highly regarded St. Louis defense, he was more confident on the mound. "I'm not going to overpower anybody," says Tudor. "I'm the kind of pitcher who has to keep the ball in play, and knowing the Cardinals' defense was behind me really helped."

How does a good defense make a pitcher better? "When you know the people behind you can catch the ball—take a double away in the outfield or go into the hole and throw a man out—you don't have to be perfect," says California Angels' hurler Dan Petry. "Having confidence in my infielders and outfielders, I don't have to be as fine with my pitches. That means I cut down the number of walks I give up, and when you cut down the walks, you give the other team less chance to score."

Petry's former manager, Sparky Anderson, has always led teams known for their prowess at the plate but says, "I'd rank defense as more important than hitting." Recent statistics indicate he may have a point. In 1982, the Chicago White Sox were ranked 13th out of the 14 American League teams in defense. After that season, the Sox hired former fielding great Ed Brinkman to tutor their infielders. In 1983, the Sox jumped to third in team defense, making 34 fewer errors, and won their division. Tudor's 1985 pennant-winning Cardinals had the best defense in baseball, with a .983 fielding percentage (meaning they successfully handled over 98 percent of all fielding chances), while the world champion Royals were right behind them at .980.

Every year, the best fielder at each position in either league as selected by the managers and coaches, wins a Gold Glove

award. In 1985, many of the winners were also among the batting leaders—the Cards' center fielder Willie McGee, the
New York Yankees' first baseman Don Mattingly and right
fielder Dave Winfield, Atlanta's center fielder Dale Murphy,
and Kansas City's third baseman George Brett.

Ask many of these ball players to talk about their offensive
production and their eyes glaze over as they deliver their
stock answers to what they feel are stock questions. But ask
them about their defense, ask them how to watch them when
they are not at the plate but in the field, and their eyes light
up. Here is the mighty Dave Winfield, after waxing poetical-
ly, albeit lengthily, on the art of playing the outfield: "I'm
sorry, I'm probably telling you more than you ever wanted to
know, but I really love to talk about this stuff."

The Tigers' second baseman Lou Whitaker, winner of three
consecutive Gold Gloves, also loves to talk about defense. But
he wonders if anybody is listening. "Unless you make a
sensational play, no one really cares," he says.

Actually, *coaches* care less about sensational plays than
simple ones. "The key to good defense is making the routine
play. All I ask of my players is to make the routine play on a
day-to-day basis," says Brinkman, a former Gold Glove
shortstop. "Anything outstanding is just a plus for you."

Brinkman agrees with Whitaker's lament that the average
fan fails to appreciate the day-to-day work of the fielder. Ever
the iconoclast, Brett, tongue-in-cheek, disagrees. "Do fans
underestimate the importance of good defense? I don't think
so. I know every time I make an error, the people sitting behind third base let me know about it!"

Always regarded as one of the top hitters in the game, Brett
is proud to have finally earned his first Gold Glove after 13
years in the big leagues. "Defense has never come easy for
me," he admits. Brett plays third base the way a fullback
rather than a halfback carries a football, the way a power
forward rumbles to the basketball hoop. Relying on intensity
and competitive spirit rather than finesse, he lacks the
smoothness of, say, a Smith or a Whitaker, who seem to be

naturals in the field. But is there really such a thing as a "natural"?

Whitaker has heard himself described that way but doesn't like the term. "I try to make everything come naturally, but there really isn't anything in this game that comes naturally," he says. "You have to work at it, and that's something I do not take lightly. For example, backhands aren't easy, so in practice I take a lot of ground balls hit to my backhand."

Whitaker was actually a third baseman who converted to second base after the Tigers indicated that the move would hasten his rise to the big leagues. Closer to the hitter than any other infielder, a third baseman needs good hands and must be able to react immediately to the batted ball; a second baseman must cover far more ground. "I always had great range to my right, and at third base you're only two steps from the bag," says Whitaker. "But I really had to work at going to my left at second base. I always watched [the Royals' superb second baseman] Frank White when I had a chance so I could see how he went to his left as well as he did. I watched and watched and asked questions. It took me some time, but I finally got it." Only after he had mastered the fundamentals of his new position did Whitaker add the dash of panache that now characterizes his game. "You have to have some style," he says with a smile.

The stylish Smith, too, has heard his admirers rave about his natural ability. "The biggest thing with not only shortstops, but all defense, is quickness—quick feet, quick hands," he says. "People say I've been blessed with those, but I still have to work hard to maintain quickness by doing certain drills. To quicken my hands, I take a lot of ground balls hit hard right at me from a short distance. I do that throughout the season."

Come out to the ball park early and watch fielding practice. The top defensive players all stand humbly at their positions fielding ground ball after ground ball or fly ball after fly ball so that come game time, 99 percent of the "routine" balls hit to them will indeed be routine. Among the hardest workers you will see are 1985 National League Most Valuable Player McGee and 1985 American League M.V.P. Mattingly.

One might think McGee could survive by his bat alone. He hit a league-leading .353 in '85. But he is not content to be known simply as a fine hitter. "I work hard at everything I do in life, whatever it may be," he says. "Defense is very important. I don't just want to be a one-dimensional player. It's a challenge when you get to a point where you think you've mastered one part of the game and then you want to move on and develop another area of your game. I work on my defense just as hard as I work on my hitting, just as hard as a pitcher works on his pitching. That means going out every day and taking line drives, fly balls, ground balls until it becomes second nature to you and it's built into you so you just react to a ball."

Mattingly observes the same work ethic and can't fathom why certain major leaguers are lax about defense. "Defense is something you can play well every day," he insists. "You're not always gonna hit. You're not always gonna feel good on offense. But you can always play good defense. And to me there's no excuse for not playing good defense. I think it's something you have to work on. It doesn't come easy. You just have to put a lot of time in. Really, playing good defense to me is *wanting* to play good defense. There are some guys who don't put as much time into it as they could. They don't put the importance on it they should."

Mattingly's preparation, like the preparation of all good fielders, is mental as well as physical: "There are plays you have to make, certain balls you do certain things with, situations where you do certain things. You need to go over in your mind what you're going to do with the ball. All the time. You start doing it in spring training. Ask, 'What do I do in this situation?' Then you just keep reminding yourself what you're gonna do with the ball when you get it."

Before every pitch Mattingly regards all the possibilities. "You need to know what you're going to do on every play. I'm thinking what I'm going to do if the ball is hit easy, if it's hit hard right at me, if it's a slow roller. If there's a play in the outfield, what am I going to do?"

While digging a low throw out of the dirt is a difficult play for a first baseman ("You practice that, but it's one you either make or don't make," says a philosophical Mattingly), fielding a well-placed sacrifice bunt can create more havoc. "The bunt play where you have to throw the ball to second base is the one that gives me the most trouble," says Mattingly. "Rushing in from first, you're blind to the play. You can rely on the catcher to tell you whether to throw to second or first, but it's something you can develop into knowing yourself, too. You must know the base runner and the speed he has. You need to have a clock in your head to know how far he is to second by the time you get the ball. Is the ball bunted hard? Did the guy get a good jump? That's the one thing you can't tell because your back is to the runner—did he get a good jump?"

The clock that ticks in every good fielder's head is set in part by scouting reports and coaches. Before a series begins, an advance scout will provide his team with information about the new opponent. The data includes where players are hitting the ball and how they are doing on the base paths. The manager or a coach will then relay the findings to their charges. As a coach with the White Sox, Jim Leyland, now manager of the Pittsburgh Pirates, earned a reputation as one of the best at interpreting scouts' findings and positioning his fielders. Every afternoon as he hit ground balls and fly balls in practice, he would talk with each fielder about how to defend against each opponent, even discussing what to do on different counts. During the game further adjustments would be made based on how the team's pitcher was throwing. Keep your eye on the dugout, and sooner or later you're bound to see a coach grab a white towel and wave it furiously. He's not signaling surrender, but rather trying to get the attention of an outfielder to align him in accordance with these observations. "It's very rewarding to see a ball hit exactly where you've placed an outfielder," says Leyland. "The average fan may not realize the preparation that's gone into this."

As useful as scouting reports may be, they are not definitive. "You have to know the players, their tendencies, if they're gonna bunt, where they're going to hit the ball, where to play," says Gold Glove third baseman Tim Wallach of the Montreal Expos. "Scouting reports are helpful, but sometimes you have different pitchers, different circumstances and guys will do different things. You just gotta learn what they do in different situations."

How do you learn? After a team takes batting practice, many of its players will repair to the clubhouse to relax before the game begins. But not the Yankees' Winfield and other students of good defense. Says Winfield: "I like to watch a guy in batting practice, learn his strengths, see what he's trying to do." Winfield's studies continue throughout a game and season. "You watch a batter at home plate in a lot of different situations. If a guy is trying to punch the ball to right, I play very shallow. Late in the game, I play deeper, because they're trying to go deep. So you just watch and anticipate what's going to happen. If a man is on base, anticipate what is about to happen, what can happen, and more times than not it does happen and you're prepared for it."

The fan who watches a Wallach or Winfield closely should learn not only what the scouting report says or what the fielder is anticipating but also the kind of pitch to be thrown and the desired location of that pitch. Says former great Reggie Jackson, "Oh, yes, you can tell a fast ball or breaking ball by the way the fielders move before the pitch reaches home plate." Very simply, if a breaking ball is to be thrown to a right-handed pull hitter, for example, then the infield will shift toward the third-base line. If a fastball is coming, the fielders will inch toward the first-base line, anticipating that the batter may swing late and hit to the right side of the field.

And how do the fielders know what the pitch is going to be? "I can usually read the catcher's signs," says shortstop

Smith, who admits to having some trouble at night if the visibility isn't good. The second baseman can also read the signs. First basemen can usually determine the pitch when right-handed batters are up (left-handed batters obstruct their view of the catcher) and third basemen can see the signs when lefties are at the plate. However, as right-handers are more likely to hit to third and left-handers to first, it's more important for these fielders to know about the signs they can't see. Here shortstops and second basemen serve as middlemen, telegraphing the sign to their fellow infielders.

When Jackson says he can tell what a pitch will be, he means he can tell when he is sitting in the dugout or the stands watching the fielders, not at the plate, where attention must be focused on the pitcher. The better defensive players never give any clues to the man with the bat. "I wait until our pitcher goes into his delivery," says Whitaker, "that way I won't tip the batter what's coming because it's hard for him to be watching me and trying to pick up the ball. I also wait because in this game you've got coaches watching every play, every move, watching the infielders trying to pick up key points to take away whatever you've got going, to try to steal those signs. I know, because we do it all the time ourselves."

Adds Wallach, "I won't usually change my position. I'll just try and get myself a better start. If a pitch is a breaking pitch and I think the batter might pull it more, I might break as the pitch is on the way. I won't do anything before that."

Fighting the tide again, Brett won't do anything, period. "I know a lot of third basemen move on certain pitches, but I don't like to know what's coming. Why? It seems like every time I move over they hit it right where I was, just out of reach. I finally gave up on the idea."

If you do see a highly regarded infielder reposition himself before a pitch, he may have something up his sleeve. Says Smith, "Sometimes you can actually intimidate the hitter into doing certain things a little early. For instance, if you go over into the hole, a right-handed batter might think a curveball is coming, when actually a fastball is coming. There are a lot of games that can be played on the field." (Smith and other wily infielders like to play another game after a ball is hit to the outfield and a runner approaches the base they are covering. They will stand nonchalantly by the bag, glove at side, and try to decoy the runner into thinking no throw is forthcoming, when in fact the ball is on its way. If a runner slows down because he thinks there is no play at the base, he may find himself thrown out when, at the last second, the prankster puts up his glove and takes the throw. "It really can work, and I'll try it every now and then," says Smith. "It's a great play if you pull it off, but unfortunately not everybody goes for the 'okey-doke.'")

While infielders actually know what the pitch is going to be, outfielders rely more on location and a sense of what their pitchers throw in certain situations. "I can tell from the way the catcher is positioned *where* a pitch is going to be thrown, but I can't read the catcher's signs to tell *what* pitch is going to be thrown," says Dwight Evans, the Boston Red Sox's long-time Gold Glove right fielder. On occasion Evans will receive help from his infield. "If we have a pitcher who throws a lot of breaking pitches or change-ups, I may get the sign from our second baseman," he says. (If a breaking ball is being thrown to a right-handed hitter, Evans would probably move toward center field.)

Winfield follows not only the location of the pitch but the sequence of the pitcher. "You know what your man is throwing," he says. "For example, you know a guy isn't going to hit a [former pitcher] Joe Niekro knuckleball too far. Or if it's a pitcher who stays on the outside part of the plate to right-handers, I can look for the ball coming my way."

Yes, agrees Evans, but you better have a reliable pitcher. "With a Luis Tiant or Bill Lee on the mound [former Red Sox pitchers], someone with good control, I knew what they were trying to do, knew exactly where they were throwing the ball. Of course, I have to know my pitchers. You can't do that if a pitcher doesn't have control."

Armed with such knowledge, Evans, unlike the infielder

who finds waiting more prudent, actually takes off before the delivery. "I can get a one or two step jump and make a play look easy," he says.

Can a fan watching Evans predict a pitch? "Yes," says the outfielder. "If a fan watches me closely, he can tell what kind of pitch is coming. But very few fans watch me, because the main attraction is at the plate."

Could a hitter see him take a head start and then guess where a pitch is coming? "I've heard some say they can, but to be watching me and watching the ball at the same time, it would take three eyes," says Evans.

When an Ozzie Smith moves in the infield or a Dwight Evans moves in the outfield, he always makes sure to communicate with his teammates. "When you move you should move as a team," says Smith. "There's a lot of communication going on out on the field. If I move, I'm going to tell my third baseman, and in turn he tells me."

Adds Evans, "We're communicating in the outfield all the time. For positioning, we have hand signs. I can make a sign with my glove to our centerfielder, and he knows exactly what I mean, or I can 'say' something to my leftfielder and he understands. We don't actually talk; we get each other's attention by whistling."

Fielders communicate with one another not only for positioning but also to remind each other of the situation and their respective responsibilities. "You always have to be in the game, watching the scoreboard to know how many outs there are, thinking what you're going to do with the ball in a certain situation," says Willie McGee. "I might tell a younger outfielder like Vince Coleman something, even though he might know it. For example, I might remind him to throw the ball to second base to keep the double play in order or hit the cutoff man. You want him thinking about what he's doing."

Focus on the second baseman and shortstop (particularly when a runner is on first base), and you will see them talking or giving each other signs between virtually every pitch.

Among other things, the tandem must determine who will cover second base if a force out or double-play ball is hit and who is going to the base if the base runner tries to steal. Then they must relay this information to the catcher and their fellow infielders.

It would seem logical that if a left-handed batter is up, the shortstop would cover second base and if a right-handed hitter is at the plate the second baseman would be responsible, because a lefty is more apt to hit to the second baseman's side and a righty is more apt to hit to the shortstop's side. More often than not, this is the case. But not always. "It's really dictated by who's hitting at the particular time," says Smith. "If there's a guy at the plate who we feel may hit and run in a situation—and we know that pretty much from our scouting reports—then we may change the signs. Then I may cover instead of our second baseman or he might do it when I normally would." (When a team tries to hit and run, the batter is trying to hit the ball in the gap vacated by the anticipated move of, say, the second baseman to the base. But if Smith rather than the second baseman covers, the strategy is foiled.)

Adds Whitaker, "Who covers second base on a steal? Who the hitter is determines that. The shortstop and I need to know if the man at the plate is a dead pull hitter, or can he go the other way. In some situations we may change to try and play a guessing game with the other team, try to do something different in different games."

Whitaker and Tigers' shortstop Alan Trammell, himself a Gold Glove winner, have played together so long that, like twins, they seem to sense each other's moves before they happen. When that kind of telepathy exists, fielders can play all sorts of tricks. Example: during a game against the White Sox in 1986, the California Angels' Reggie Jackson stole second base. The catcher's throw to second baseman Julio Cruz was low, and to the fan and the sliding Jackson alike, it appeared that the ball had scooted past Cruz into center field. Cruz perpetuated this notion by pounding the earth in disgust, and at the same time Sox shortstop Ozzie Guillen ran into the outfield, apparently to retrieve the errant throw. Jackson rose and almost left the safe haven of the base to head to third, then stopped and laughed, aware now that the second baseman and shortstop (without ever having said a word to one another) had almost fooled him. Cruz had caught the ball and possessed it the whole time.

Such shenanigans make the game more fun, but in the long run it is the ability to execute the fundamentals that separate the good defenders from the mediocre ones. Every time a ball is hit, a ballet of sorts occurs, with each fielder performing in a manner choreographed long ago on the practice field. This is most evident and most interesting to watch on a base hit to the outfield with a runner on base. Imagine that with the Royals' speedy Willie Wilson on second base against the Yankees, George Brett strokes a hit to right field. Right fielder Winfield moves quickly to the ball, while center fielder Claudell Washington moves behind him to back him up if the ball gets past. Winfield appears to have a chance to throw Wilson out as he heads for home. But if the throw is late, then Brett, who would ordinarily stop at first, will move to second and be in scoring position himself. First baseman Mattingly, called "the cutoff man" in this situation, positions himself in a direct line between Winfield and home plate, where catcher Joel Skinner stands ready for the throw, and where, behind the plate, pitcher Ron Guidry is ready to retrieve a wild heave. (Yes, the pitcher is involved. Indeed, the left fielder may also be involved, backing up third base in case a throw there becomes necessary.) Shortstop Wayne Tolleson has moved to cover second base, while second baseman Willie Randolph has moved to the edge of the outfield to field the throw should Winfield determine he has no play on Wilson. But Winfield does think he has a play. His job now? Throw the ball in such a line that Mattingly can either catch the ball—cut it off—and then prevent Brett from taking second base or let the ball go through to nail Wilson at the plate. Mattingly makes the final decision based on his observations and the observations of his catcher and fellow fielders.

This play or a more complicated variation (say, a base hit with runners on first and second) is bound to happen in every game. If the team in the field fails to execute it properly day in and day out, doesn't hit the cutoff man 99 percent of the time, it can be quite harmful. "You check the standings," says Haywood Sullivan, a former catcher and managing partner of the Boston Red Sox. "It's the teams who can execute the fundamentals that are at the top every year."

Whether a Willie Wilson tries to take an extra base on an outfielder depends on his own speed, the speed of the outfielder in reaching the ball, and the outfielder's arm. As the center fielder must cover more ground than the men on his left and right, speed is a prerequisite at that position. "The key to playing center field is speed," McGee acknowledges. "But a guy can have a lot of speed and run by balls, so you have to put in hard work to know which balls you can get to, to know how to come in on line drives, how to react on balls hit over your head."

How does a center fielder judge a ball hit toward him? "It's just a matter of being relaxed and getting a good jump on the ball," says McGee. "You're taught to freeze on a ball when it's hit so you can make your judgment. But if the batter is someone with great power like [the Cards'] Pedro Guerrero, you're looking to go back, and if it's a guy you know is a line-drive hitter, then you know that 80 percent of the time he's not going to hit it over your head and you're prepared to go in. A line-drive hit straight at you at eye level is the hardest ball to judge because it has a tendency to take off on you. And sometimes the big, strong guys hit the ball so hard it comes out there like a knuckleball and is really tough."

Just as a center fielder like McGee must learn to control his speed so he doesn't overrun balls, a right fielder like Winfield must learn to control his arm. "I always knew I had a real good arm, so I always liked to display it if I caught the ball. You're better off having a good arm than not having it," he says, laughing. "But you have to do everything under control. It's like hitting. You can have a lot of power, but if you're not under control, it doesn't do you that much good."

Winfield takes great pains to avoid getting great pains in the arm. "I've taken care of it over the years," he says. "Some people will throw it out because they don't know how to take care of themselves. Always warm up, loosen up. If it's hurt, don't keep pushing it, give it some rest. Display it when you need to. Sometimes you can go on *reputation.*" He pauses, then lest any runners mistake his meaning, adds, "But I still have the arm and I like right field because I can display it. I really enjoy preventing a runner from going from first to third, and when I throw a guy out, I get a big kick out of it. You know, you just have to take pride in your defense."

Winfield, who has played left field and center field, too, prefers right. "I don't like throwing from left," he says. "You have a different perspective throwing to home with the runner rounding third and coming home. When you're in right field and the ball is hit out there, the runner who was on second is just about to reach third base and you see where the catcher is and see where the runner is and it's just a much calmer and better perspective on throwing, so you're much more under control. You can tell from the outfield whether or not you're going to get him before you make the play. In left field you can't."

The Red Sox's Evans is, like Winfield, best known for his arm. He terms being able to throw well "a God-given talent," and doubts that outfielders can turn an average arm into a great one by exercise or anything else. But a great arm, he insists, is not enough. "There are so many other things going on in the field [besides throwing]," he says. "Catching the ball and fundamentals like the way you charge the ball, your footwork after you catch the ball so you can throw it well. Situations: keeping the ball in front of you, getting the jump, keeping the ball out of the sun."

Right field seems to be the sun field in most ball parks, Boston's Fenway Park among them. But as difficult as it is to find the ball in the sun, says Evans, it is even more difficult to find it at night. "I would rather battle the sun on a fly ball than the lights. You can learn to position yourself with the sun; it's only so big when you're under a ball. But the lights take up almost the whole field; it's harder to get around them. It's very difficult to see."

Even if a ball can be seen, it is not as easy to catch as it might appear. "A lot of fans think a line drive hit to right field comes right at you, but it doesn't," says Evans. "If a left-hander is hitting, the ball usually hooks toward the line. But then you'll get a few lefties who put a weird swing on the ball and it breaks toward center field. Our Rich Gedman is like that. I've only seen a few others—Tony Oliva and Cecil Cooper. Then you get someone like (the Montreal Expos') Graig Nettles who's got that upswing on the ball, and just as it looks like you've got it, all of a sudden it just bites right down and is in front of you. That can make you look foolish out there. It's experience, knowing how the ball comes off the bat of different players. There's a lot of homework involved. You don't just go out there and play."

Even the park makes a difference to a fielder. "Definitely," says Evans. "In Fenway Park, there's no foul territory. In other parks like Oakland, you have a tremendous amount of foul territory to cover. In right field in Yankee Stadium everything is actually downhill. When you throw, it's like throwing off the mound. To me that's the easiest right field."

When Ozzie Smith was traded to the Cardinals by the San Diego Padres before the 1982 season, many in the baseball world thought St. Louis's artificial turf infield would be difficult for him. "When I came to St. Louis, a lot of people thought I wouldn't get to a lot of balls that I would have been able to get on grass," since the ball moves much faster through an artificial turf infield. Two pennants, one world championship, and several Gold Gloves later, Smith can smile when he says, "That was a myth. I've been able to cover as much ground, if not more, by learning the positioning of guys. As you get older, the more you play the game, the more you learn about hitters."

From an esthetic standpoint, almost every major leaguer prefers the idea of natural grass as opposed to artificial turf, but when it comes to fielding the ball, many infielders prefer the turf. Says Tim Wallach, "I prefer natural grass, but I don't want to take a ball in the face because of a bad hop. Obviously you get truer bounces on the turf."

Situated at third base, the hot corner, Wallach must stare down the barrel of a bat that can propel a ball at great speed. Does he ever worry about taking a line drive in the face? "No, I'm not scared. I feel I'm quick enough so that if I am going to be hit, it's gonna be in the chest, not the face. That's part of the game, so it doesn't bother me."

A former outfielder, Wallach developed into a respected in-fielder thanks in large part to the instruction he received from former infielders Bill Mazeroski and Ron Hansen, an Expos coach. Virtually every ball club has instructors at spring train-ing and coaches at the major-league level to work with fielders. What can a coach do? "Most fielders field the ball correctly most of the time, but once in awhile they'll get into a rut," says Eddie Brinkman. "An infielder might be pulling his head up too soon, thinking about a throw before he picks the ball up, or he might be positioning his feet too close together. I'll pick this up and mention it to him."

Sometimes a coach must be a counselor as well. "People talked about the improvement in our defense," says Brinkman. "Well, the players had the talent in the first place. But they'd read how terrible they were and were starting to believe it. I had to get their confidence back. I'd say, 'Hey, we know you can play. It's just a matter of going out and doing it.' Once they start making the plays, they realize they're not so bad after all, and it carries over from one guy to the next."

If a team or an individual can develop a reputation for good defense, the opposition may be forced to alter its approach to particular situations. Runners think twice about trying to take the extra base on Winfield or Evans; base stealers are reluctant to challenge the arm of a Gold Glove catcher like Lance Parrish. Some teams are even afraid to bunt when the Yankees' Ron Guidry is pitching. "Normally, guys don't bunt on a pitcher who has a reputation for being fast and a good fielder, and I have that reputation," says Guidry, who in addition to winning 22 games in 1985 won the Gold Glove. "So a lot of good bunters won't bunt because they almost have to make a perfect bunt on me to get on."

Fans don't normally think about the fielding ability of a pitcher, but pitchers do. "As a pitcher, defense to you is a majority of the ball game," says Guidry. "They say games are won on pitching and defense and that means you have to be able to field your position well because you will have a lot of balls that are hit up the middle. A lot of times a good pitcher with some speed, a guy who can move from the left or right off the mound, can cut the ground balls off. Other times, there are plays that require you to move quickly to the line on both sides of the diamond. Say you're pitching and the guy hits a little swinging chopper down the third-base line and the third baseman is playing back. He won't be able to get it, but if you can field your position well and are quick enough and agile enough to get off the mound, you can make the play at first base. That's a big play, because if the next guy gets a base hit you'd have been faced with a first-and-second-or-third situation. That's what fielding does for you. It will make the offense have to hit the ball to score runs, and that's the name of the game."

Guidry's teammate Mattingly talks about contemplating all the fielding variables. One would think that a pitcher would be so preoccupied with getting the batter out that he would have little time to think about what he is going to do with a ground ball, what base he should cover if the ball is hit to right field. Says Guidry, "Your main concern is just pitching and getting the guy out. After you've played the game many years, your instincts take over. Very seldom when I'm pitching do I think about the guy chopping the ball or hitting it up the middle, because if it does occur, your instincts will make you move to wherever the ball is. So you don't really worry about all the things that can go on, because if you do worry you're gonna omit something. You're gonna omit trying to get the guy at the plate out. And he's still the most important guy. He still has to hit the ball to be able to make the other guys go."

While Guidry makes fielding his position sound largely instinctive, he sounds downright analytical when describing two plays a pitcher must make, covering first base and fielding the sacrifice bunt.

Here's Guidry on each play:

Covering first. "If a ball is hit very slowly down to first base, most of the time I'll get those. If it's a ball that's hit hard, either the first baseman or second baseman will get it. If it's hard enough for the second baseman to get, then the first baseman will cover, but if the first baseman has to get it, I'll be in position because I'm moving over there to cover first. One of the hardest plays is when the ball is hit intermediately, where I can't get it and the first baseman has to come in in back of me and make a quick play. But most of the time when that happens my speed lets me get there in enough time so that the first baseman doesn't have to throw the ball hard or quick. He can just get it, take his time and he'll get the guy because I'm quick, so not too many runners will beat me over there."

The sacrifice bunt. "You rely on your catcher to give you a good idea, but you know through experience whether to throw to first base. That's based on the situation, who's running. If you have a fast guy on first and if it's a bunt where the first baseman and third baseman are charging and you're moving up the middle, by the time I release the pitch, I'm gonna be moving. If the guy bunts the ball directly to me hard, then I can have a chance at second base. If it's bunted slowly where I have to run up far, then I gotta go to first base. I'm not gonna take a chance on the guy going to second. If it's bunted to the third baseman or first baseman, then I'm out of the play. If the third baseman is back, then I have to get to the third-base line, so if it's a good bunt there I have no other play than to go to first. Or say if the guy is on second and they're trying to get him to third base, well, I have to get to the line. If I get there quickly then I have a shot at third base. And the catcher will let you know because he's watching. If I get the ball and the runner is 10 feet from third base, then I have a chance to get him, so the catcher will holler as soon as the ball and I get almost to the same spot. He won't holler once I pick it up, because by then it's too late. He has to let me know when I'm in the process."

As the words of the other fielders indicate, the pitcher is not the only man who relies on the catcher at some point during the game. The third baseman or first baseman requires his help on the bunt; the second baseman and shortstop rely on him to get the signs; the outfielders watch him to determine pitch location. And the whole team needs him to stand guard at the plate not only to block pitches in the dirt, but to block runners trying to score. (The vastly different worlds of baseball and football seem to intersect at home plate in the person of the catcher, the only defender to wear a helmet and to block.)

"Just about anybody you talk to in baseball will say the number-one preference is that a catcher be good defensively," says Lance Parrish, who turned down a football scholarship at UCLA to sign with the Tigers, and at 6'3" 220 pounds looks more like a Mike Ditka-type tight end than a Yogi Berra-type catcher. Parrish, like his former teammate Whitaker, was originally a third baseman; he, too, changed positions because he didn't want to wait for the retirement of then Tigers' third baseman Aurelio Rodriguez (who incidentally was treasured more for his glove than his bat).

Although he has won several Gold Gloves, Parrish agrees with Whitaker that few things in baseball are natural. "I don't think defense comes easily to anybody," he says. "It takes time to learn the position. It's difficult because you're working out of a squat position most of the time. You have to learn how to receive pitches properly, how to turn the ball into the strike zone, how to block pitches in the dirt. There are so many things involved; it takes time."

The interested fan should watch the catcher's feet for a few pitches. "The crucial thing is weight distribution," explains Parrish. "You always have to be on the balls of your feet. You can't catch on your heels, because you just can't move. You have to be able to move left and right, but you can't do that unless you're evenly balanced and comfortable there."

Blocking pitches may be the most underappreciated skill in the game. If the catcher allows a pitch to get past him when there is a runner on base, the runner may very well advance. The effect, then, is the same as a base hit or a walk. For years Carlton Fisk, the White Sox All-Star catcher, has kept a statistic that even the growing legion of baseball statisticians has yet to add to their canon: pitches blocked that result in runs saved (perhaps no one has kept this stat because PBTRIRS would fill up half the box score), but next time you are scoring a game, make a mark each time the man behind the plate blocks a pitch, then determine at the end of the inning how crucial each block was). Fisk provides a description: "These are balls in the dirt that you throw yourself in front of and that hit you in the neck or wherever and the runner doesn't advance and it saves a run. He could be on first base and the next guy gets a hit and then the next guy hits a fly ball that would have scored him. In 1985, I saved our club 221 runs. And that wasn't my best. Some years the pitchers are more reliable than others. One year when I was with Boston, I saved 287 runs. I've always felt that was my most important role."

In addition to blocking pitches, the catcher must be prepared to block the plate when a runner attempts to score. The problem here is one of timing. The catcher cannot block the runner's path until he actually has the ball. If the ball is coming from left field, the catching must wait helplessly as the runner, whom he can see clearly, barrels in on a potential collision course. If the ball is coming in from right field, the catcher, except for a few hasty peeks, is unable to see the runner. Upon finally catching the ball, he must secure it, pivot to tag the runner, guard the plate, and, of course, hold onto the ball while the runner attempts to kick or knock it out of his glove. In 1985, Fisk was involved in one of the weirdest plays in baseball history when he tagged out two Yankees, Bobby Meacham and Dale Berra, at the plate on the same play. It's bad enough to have one runner fighting for the plate. What goes through a catcher's mind as double trouble approaches? "It was the most bizarre play I've ever been involved in," Fisk recalls. "The ball was hit to left center, and I saw them both stacking up at second base and then Ozzie [Sox shortstop Ozzie Guillen] got the relay throw and I knew Meacham was coming and I happened to glance down and saw both of them coming. I knew the second guy was coming. I just didn't know what the interval was. If he'd have been a little closer or if I'd have let Meacham stack me up, I'd have missed him." Fisk is lucky he escaped injury on that play. Earlier in the season the Dodgers' Mike Scioscia, perhaps the most fearless when it comes to standing his ground, was knocked cold.

Thus it is that Parrish provides the following job description: "Catchers have to be the type of people that want to be in control of situations and enjoy pain! And are able to play with pain. I can honestly say catchers are expected to play with pain. It's almost a miracle if you can go for any length of time without having something wrong with you. You just have to learn to play with it. Whether it's your hands, your knees, or your arms, it's always something. Squatting takes its toll on you, too. I have a problem with my knee sometimes, with my lower back. You just have to do the necessary things to take care of those problems.

"I can lose anywhere from five to ten pounds on a really hot day. I've come off the field a few times when there was not a dry spot on me. I've actually had to go into the clubhouse and change my uniform because every time I touched myself I couldn't find a dry spot to wipe my hands.

"Conditioning is a must. You have to take care of your body, have to do a lot of stretching, have to do exercises to try and strengthen certain areas. That's just part of the ritual."

Does Fisk think the average fan is aware of what the catcher goes through? "I'm afraid much of it goes unnoticed because it's not spectacular," he says. "It's not a home run; it's not a double; it's not a dive. You could block seven balls and save seven runs a game all year long, but nobody would ever notice. Then a guy comes along and hits a home run and everybody thinks he's a good ball player."

And so we have come full circle from the lament of Lou Whitaker that fans only appreciate the sensational. So if the roar of the crowd doesn't motivate the player, what does?

Fisk remembers another game against the Yankees in which he saved several runs. "After it was over, Jeff Torborg [a former catcher and coach with the Yankees] came up to me and said, 'You really put on a catching clinic.' And that makes it all worthwhile, when you're recognized by your peers as doing the job you're supposed to do."

Adds Winfield, "If you're worth your salt, you have to feel you're one of the best. I'm proud that I've won the Gold Glove. It does mean a lot. You get one and you want more."

5

BASE STEALING: THE GUESSING GAME

Consider, no *savor*, the stolen base. Where else in sport can a team advance its cause so dramatically and effectively without touching the ball? The mere anticipation of such thievery is enough to bring fans to the edge of their seats and cause television directors to "split" the screen so that those at home may watch both batter and runner. The ballpark comes alive when a Rickey Henderson or a Vince Coleman takes his mark (a daring 4 1/2 step lead off), then gets set on legs poised like two tightly strung bows. Pitchers and hitters may play the game with confidence and control. Base stealers seem possessed of cockiness and uncontainable energy.

Who invented basestealing?

The historians at the Hall of Fame are baffled, although they can find mention of such skullduggery dating back to 1862. *The Spaulding Guide*, baseball's statistical bible, started recording the ploy in 1887, but in those days credit was also given for "stealing" an extra base—say, moving from first to third—on a hit. This inflation, which lasted until 1898, accounts for the eye-opening 129 steals amassed by Arlie Latham in 1887. (Latham, who played for St. Louis, can also lay claim to one of the game's longest and most intriguing nicknames; he was called "The Freshest Man on Earth.")

"The Georgia Peach," Ty Cobb, was the most celebrated of the modern-era base thieves, and his lifetime record of 892 steals lasted 49 years until surpassed by Lou Brock in 1977. Brock, who retired with 938 thefts, may be overtaken more quickly. The New York Yankees' Henderson, who stole a single-season record 130 bases in 1982; the St. Louis Cardinals' Coleman, who as a rookie in 1985 swiped 110 bases; and the Montreal Expos' Tim Raines, who led the National League in each of his first four seasons before Coleman arrived, are all destined to mount serious challenges. They are representative of a new generation of base stealers, spawned in part by the installation of artificial turf. Tom Seaver, the great pitcher, wrote his college thesis on the effect of the playing surface on the game: "Astroturf created the need for overall speed, especially in the outfield," he explained to me last season. "And soon this defensive speed was transferred to offensive speed. This is one of the biggest changes I've seen in the game."

Seaver says that the stolen base "is definitely more important than when I first came up," and statistics bear him out. In 1967, his rookie season, a total of 1,373 bases were stolen by the 20 major-league teams. In 1988 the 26 clubs accounted for well over 3,000 steals.

The numbers seem likely to continue to increase. While some proponents of sabermetrics, the mathematical and statistical analysis of baseball, have recently argued that the stolen base is an overrated and overused strategy that does not produce runs often enough to justify its risk, most baseball practitioners remain enamored of it. For not only does the successful steal have the potential to wreak havoc by advancing a runner into scoring position, the mere *threat* of the steal produces changes in the defense and pitching that can be even more beneficial.

Says Joe Morgan, who retired after the 1984 season as the 10th leading base stealer in history: "The threat of the stolen base can be very intimidating." Here, the bark may be worse than the bite.

What happens when a player who's a stealing threat reaches base? "The infield gets jumpy, because it doesn't know what's going to happen," says Morgan. "The hitter gains an advantage because the catcher calls for more fastballs so he'll have a better chance of throwing the runner out. And the pitcher has to divide his concentration between the batter and the man at first base." At the same time, the first baseman, customarily several strides away, relocates to hold the runner close to the base. This opens up the infield for the hitter.

These are the circumstances a manager likes to create and then exploit. In 1983, the Chicago Cubs stole 84 bases, 40 fewer than any other National League team, and finished 71-91, second worst in the league. After the season, the Cubs hired a new manager, Jim Frey, who believes in the running game, and acquired the speedy center fielder Bobby Dernier to bat leadoff and cause a commotion on the base paths. Despite an injury, Dernier stole 45 bases; the team stole 154 bases; and the Cubs gained a spot in post-season play for the first time in 39 years.

Frey, who was named Manager of the Year in '84 (he was then fired in 1986), attributed much of the club's turnaround to its new-found aggressiveness and pays no heed to the rattling of the sabermetricians. "The computer people have no understanding of the psychological, the human element of the game," he says. "What they don't understand is that you're dealing with 25 individuals, most of whom like to play an aggressive game. Nobody likes to be known as a 'safety first' player. My teams have always enjoyed having the image of being aggressive, and having that image has always had an effect on the opposition."

Imitating the '84 Cubs were the '85 Yankees, who traded for their own basestealing leadoff man and center fielder, Henderson. While with the Oakland A's the previous season,

Henderson had stolen more bases than all the Yankees' players combined, and in his first year in New York he stole a league-leading 80 bases, as the Yankees, who had relied strictly on power for years, improved dramatically over 1984 and fell just short of the Toronto Blue Jays for the division championship.

Of course, just as the emperor with no clothes was eventually exposed, so, too, is the ball club or ball player unable to back up an aggressive image with real success on the bases. "I'm not impressed by the guy who has 30 stolen bases by July but has been caught 15 times," says Pittsburgh Pirates' pitching coach Ray Miller. "The strategy is only worthwhile if you're successful 70 percent of the time. Otherwise you take yourself out of too many innings." Joe Morgan sets an even higher standard: "The great base stealer should make it at least 80 percent of the time," he says.

80 percent? You're a great home run hitter if you convert considerably less than 8 percent of your opportunities, a great hitter if you make good on 30 percent of your chances. Is it that easy to steal a base? Does the advantage really rest so overwhelmingly with the runner?

Johnny Oates, a former big-league catcher, Cubs' coach, and now a minor league manager, has put a stopwatch on virtually every pitcher, catcher, and runner in the National League. "The average pitch takes about 1.3 seconds to reach the catcher's glove," Oates says. "And the average throw to second base takes about 2.0 seconds. The best runners, guys like Bobby Dernier, make it from first to second in about 3.05 or 3.1. You're going to have a tough time throwing them out, but you have to get the guys who get down there in 3.4."

Time, then, is the field on which this battle for a 90-foot advantage is fought. Pitcher and catcher work on two fronts: trying to decrease the time it takes for the ball to go from mound to plate to second base, and trying to increase the time it takes the runner to move from first to second. At the same time, the runner is in a sense trying to cheat time, trying to take off for second base before the pitcher has released the ball.

While it is an important element of the steal, speed alone does not determine whether time will favor the runner. "You can be the fastest man in baseball but not be able to steal a base unless you can analyze the pitcher," says the Cardinals' Coleman.

The Expos' Raines agrees. "When I first came up, I relied on my speed," he says. "But after four years the pitchers have begun to do different things when I get on base. They change their pitching motion. They speed up their delivery to the plate. They throw to first more often. As a result, I've been learning how to read pitchers. When I'm on base or in the dugout when someone else is on base, I study what the pitcher is doing."

"Reading a pitcher" is the art of determining whether a pitcher is going to throw to first base to pick off the runner or deliver the pitch to the batter. "This is the key to basestealing, making the pitcher commit himself to home before you've committed yourself to run," says Dave Nelson, the instructor who turned around the White Sox's fortunes on the base paths in their 1983 championship season. "Otherwise, once you're committed and he isn't, he can throw to first and you're dead."

Morgan simplifies it: "You look for the green light that says 'go' or the red light that says 'don't go.' "

When it comes to being read, some pitchers are as simple as, say, Rod McKuen, while others may be veritable James Joyces. Nelson contends that, however complicated, each pitcher eventually gives himself away. "Pitchers are creatures of habit," he says. "If you watch them long enough, you'll see a certain thing that tells you that the pitcher is going to the plate. It's at that precise moment—when you know the pitcher can't throw to first—that you accelerate and head for second base."

Nelson prefers not to give a book report on an active hurler, but he will spill the beans on Jesse Jefferson, a hard thrower who played for several American League teams between 1975 and 1981. "When Jesse was pitching for the Angels, I told my guys, 'Hey, you can steal on him,' " remembers Nelson. "He had fairly quick feet to first base, but he had this twitch in the right cheek of his behind. Every time you saw the twitch, it meant he was throwing home. He never threw to first base after he twitched. I'd tell my players to take off as soon as they saw the reflex action in the cheek."

Jefferson was a right-hander, and many young stealers who do rely primarily on speed maintain that it is easier to steal off righties because they can't see first base as well as left-handers. Nelson and Morgan disagree. "It's easier to read a left-hander because you can see everything in front of you," explains Morgan.

Nelson says that the fan who watches baseball seriously should, over time, be able to read many pitchers. "Pretend you're a runner," he advises, "and start watching the pitcher from the feet up for something to key on." Here, in his words, is what he would tell his runners to look for:

When the Pitcher Is Right-Handed

WATCH THE PITCHER'S RIGHT HEEL.

"This is the toughest way to learn how to steal a base because it demands exceptional concentration, but if you see the right heel move, it means the pitcher has to throw to first base or step off the rubber. He can't go home. It's tough to pick up, but once you do, the rest becomes automatic and you'll see a lot of other things move that will tell you what the pitcher is going to do."

WATCH THE PITCHER'S CAP.

When most right-handers are in the set position, they have difficulty judging the size of the runner's leadoff from first base. So to add to his peripheral vision, a righty will tip his head down. This lets him look over better, but you can't throw over to first from that position. Normally, the pitcher will have to lift his head. At this point his cap bill comes up. I'd tell my runners to go when they saw the cap bill rise. But you have to be careful. Some pitchers will tuck their heads, but then they'll whip their heads several times to give the runner a little fake."

WATCH THE PITCHER'S SHOULDER.

"Most pitchers set up 'open,' so, in order to throw to first, they've got to bring the left shoulder around. Also, some pitchers will lean their shoulder, just lean forward before going home."

When the Pitcher Is Left-Handed

WATCH THE PITCHER'S EYES.

"The runner can look directly at the left-hander. If you watch his eyes and head, you may be able to tell if he's worried, and that can tip off a lot of things. The basic thing most left-handers do wrong is try to fool you by looking toward home and throwing to first base."

WATCH THE PITCHER'S UPPER BODY.

"A lot of left-handers, especially the big guys, have a tendency to tilt their upper body when they're going to try a pickoff. You can see the difference in their body position. If they start straight up, then lean, tilt way back, they're coming to first base."

WATCH THE PITCHER'S LEG KICK.

"Most of the time left-handers will have a high leg kick to the plate and a short leg kick if they're coming to first base. So you can sometimes judge by the height of the kick. Another thing to look for is what is called 'breaking the plane.' When the pitcher's leg comes past the rubber, now he can't throw to first base. Some lefties like to stay right on the verge of crossing over, not really crossing, so I hope my runners will have read something else sooner to tell if the pitcher is going to home or first."

All Pitchers

WATCH THE PITCHER'S RHYTHM.

"Sometimes reading the pitcher is very simple. You don't have to worry about a head or a shoulder lean. Some pitchers are just very rhythmic. Once this kind of pitcher is set, you can count, say, to three, and the pitcher goes home. So you watch and count, and if it's the same count, say, for the first two pitches, on the third pitch you count, 'one, two, three,' then boom, you go. The key for a runner here is not to get too anxious and disrupt the pitcher's rhythm."

When one of his foot soldiers reached base, Nelson, coaching at first, quietly reminded him how to read the man on the mound. One might think that first basemen would try to eavesdrop on such conversations, but, says Nelson, "The only guy that really tries is the Orioles' Eddie Murray. He did a lot of good things like trying to overhear me and trying to distract base runners. He talks to his pitchers a lot, saying, 'Okay, throw over, throw over,' and the pitcher isn't supposed to throw over, but then he may say a key word, and the pitcher knows Eddie wants him to throw."

One thing Murray will never hear from Nelson and other first-base coaches is exactly when a runner is going to steal. "I rarely knew when a guy was going," admits Nelson. Why? Because often when managers do put on the steal, the runner has the discretion to pick the particular pitch on which to take off. Still, Nelson had a better clue than most. He kept a stopwatch in his pocket so he could time a pitcher's delivery and then signal the results back to his manager in the dugout. Five fingers, for example, meant a delivery time of 1.5 seconds. Perhaps this time would be slower than normal for the particular pitcher. The manager could then decide whether to signal the steal.

Scouting reports give the defense clues as to when a team likes to run and on what counts certain players have a tendency to steal. Cubs' catcher Jody Davis finds two balls and one strike the most popular count to run on. "The runner knows it's tough for us to pitch out then because we don't want to get further behind on the batter," he says.

Should you wait until then to look for the steal? "Not if you've got a base runner like Rickey Henderson," smiles Nelson. "I'd start watching from the first pitch."

With other runners, the number of outs and the batter may dictate strategy. Some runners are reluctant to go if the pitcher gets ahead of the batter because a pitchout becomes more likely. Others, like Raines, will go when they think a breaking pitch will be thrown because it takes longer for such a pitch to reach home plate. Some managers may signal the runner to stay put so a left-handed batter can take advantage of the positioning of the first baseman nearer the bag or because they don't want the batter taking pitches in order to give the runner a chance to steal.

The batter, who in most cases does know if the runner is going, is frequently a silent partner in a successful theft. Nelson provides the following job description for a man who bats behind a base stealer: "He has to be able to handle the bat. He has to be able to take a pitch to let the guy steal, protect the runner, and then have the ability to hit to the right side of the field to advance the runner after the steal."

There is a certain amount of sacrifice involved in batting behind a base stealer, but there is also reward. Two months into the 1983 season, White Sox catcher Carlton Fisk was mired in a terrible slump, batting under .200. Manager Tony LaRussa then moved him to the second spot in the batting order, behind the fleet Rudy Law. With Law frequently on base in front of him, Fisk of necessity became a more alert hitter. He also started seeing more fastballs, thrown in deference to Law's basestealing potential. Fisk batted well over .300 the rest of the season and dramatically increased his home runs and runs batted in. (Law also benefited from the change. After Fisk got hot, Law didn't get a lot of pitchouts because the pitchers did not want to fall behind on the count to Fisk. Law's final totals: 77 stolen bases in 89 attempts, a new team record.)

The men batting behind top base stealers continue to benefit as much as Fisk. In 1984, Ryne Sandberg followed Dernier in the Cubs' lineup, batted .314 and was selected the National League's Most Valuable Player. Sandberg was succeeded in '85 by the Cardinals' Willie McGee, who, batting after the distracting Coleman, hit a resounding .353.

Former Cubs' manager Frey and Cardinals' skipper Whitey Herzog frequently did not require their top hitters to take pitches for their top runners. Explains Frey: "If you've got a guy capable of stealing, you give him the freedom to steal. If you've got a guy hitting behind him who can hit, you give him the opportunity to do so. The advantage with a guy like Dernier on base is that he might force the pitcher to throw fastballs so Sandberg can look for that pitch and drive it."

Not making your hitter take pitches flies in the face of tradition, but according to Ray Miller, the traditionalists no longer run the running game. In the past the stolen base was utilized by managers trying to spark a big inning or just scratch out one run, but today, he says, "There's a lot of antiestablishment-type stealing. Teams steal when they have big leads and even when they are behind." Miller, who was previously the Baltimore Orioles' pitching coach, recalls a game in which the Orioles led the Indians by three runs in the ninth inning. "Cleveland's Tony Bernazard stole second. Then on the next pitch, he took off for third. We were all sitting on the bench laughing. Stealing bases in that situation isn't going to help, and the pitcher shouldn't even worry about it."

Miller will sometimes even tell his pitcher not to worry

about a runner in the late innings of a close game. "If you've got a guy who's pitching well, has maybe nine or 10 strikeouts, let him go with his game and focus on the batter. Go with the odds that he can get the men at the plate out, and let the runner steal."

Most of the time, however, the pitcher will reserve at least one eye for the runner at first base. Nelson makes reading a pitcher easy. But before holding a tag day for the seemingly helpless hurler, listen to Tom Seaver: "There are things a pitcher can do. Alter the delivery to home plate at different times to break the runner's timing. Avoid being repetitious. Maybe pitch out or throw a fastball to a location that helps the catcher if you think the runner is going. And, of course, periodically, throw to first base to keep the runner close."

Most pitchers feature a variety of moves to first base. Bill Gullickson, who played for the Reds and the Yankees before signing a lucrative contract to play in Japan, is typical. "I have three different moves," he explains. "The first is just to show the runner I can come over there. The second is my deke; I try to make the runner think that's my best. And the third is my best. You always hold that until an important time in the game when you think you can actually pick someone off."

The pickoff. If the threat of a stolen base strikes fear in the hearts of pitcher and catcher, the pickoff holds its own terror for the runner. It may be baseball's most humiliating moment when the picked-off runner, who only seconds before was dancing bravely, picks himself off the ground, with the dirt on his once-clean uniform as a red badge of futility. "It's a long walk back to the dugout after you've been nailed," says Nelson.

Baltimore's pickoff plays are representative of those employed by most other clubs. "On one, the pitcher signals the first baseman that he'll either throw over to first or step off the rubber, but he definitely won't throw home," explains Miller. "On another, the catcher initiates the pickoff by sending a signal to the pitcher. And on the third, the pitcher just throws when he sees daylight between the runner and first base."

For the right-handed pitcher, who has his back to the base, this final move is more difficult than it sounds. "I can't actually see the runner," says Gullickson. "What I see is a shadow more than a moving figure, so I can't really see how far off the base he is. I judge that based on my throw to first. If I make a pretty good move and he's just barely getting back, I get some feeling."

Runners, like pitchers, can often be read. "When the other team is up, a coaching staff will watch to see if runners tip off that they're going," says Nelson. "Sometimes they tip it off by trying to be too nonchalant; they give you this nonchalant little lead and then they're going to boom ahead."

Other times runners will take their basestealing leadoff only when they are going to try to steal. Says Nelson, "Players should be in a ready position all the time, so the other team won't know if they're going or not." Even a slower runner, Nelson says, should get a good lead. He may never steal, but he should be in a position to go from first to third—steal an extra base in the old sense—on a single.

When he was coaching, Nelson showed his runners their leadoffs on videotape and worked with them on technique in spring training. "A lot of guys take their leadoff and have no conception of where they are," he laments. "So I make them practice leading off and getting back to the base with their eyes closed." During a game, of course, those eyes must stay open, and they should be fixed on the pitcher. "Some guys creep off the base and all of a sudden they don't know where they are," says Nelson. "They've made the mistake of taking their eyes off the pitcher, the man who can pick them off, and I've seen them get caught that way."

Herzog, architect of the go-go Cardinals, also uses the exhibition season to stress good basestealing technique. "I don't want my guys to steal in spring training because they might get hurt," he says. "But I want them to work on their leads so that when the season begins they're comfortable getting the big lead. I don't really care if they get picked off in the exhibitions. In fact if a guy is a timid base runner, I want him to get picked off, want him to keep trying to find how far he can get off the base."

A good runner, then, should learn something from the attempted pickoff. "Sometimes I try to make the pitcher give me his best move so I can get a sense of how far to lead off," says Raines. "I can get a bigger lead on some pitchers than others, depending on their pickoff."

Which pitchers have the best moves? "Fernando Valenzuela," says Raines. Coleman disagrees. "Roger McDowell of the Mets."

Coleman does not include the Montreal Expos' pitcher who once threw over to first base 13 times in a row after Coleman hit the first pitch of the game for a single. When the pitcher finally threw again to home, he pitched out. Coleman was stealing, and despite the pitchout, he was safe. His reaction: "It just showed me that the pitcher wasn't confident in his own move or his catcher. I feel if he hasn't picked me off in four or five tries, he should leave it up to the catcher; that's his job. The pitcher's priority is to get the batter out. He had his chance with me when I was at the plate. Now if he wants to try and play cat and mouse with me, cut my lead, that's fine. But it isn't going to happen."

A big leadoff does not ensure a successful steal. Most of the top basestealers try to take a 4 1/2 step lead from first base, but Henderson only takes a 3 1/2 step lead. He compensates by getting what former manager Gene Mauch has called the quickest start he has ever seen. "You have to get a quick start," says Morgan, who, along with Raines and many of today's successful runners, is a proponent of taking off with the "crossover step." To achieve the same thrust a sprinter gets when coming out of the blocks, these base stealers shoot their left leg, the one closest to first base, over and around the right foot, pivot on the right, and then fly.

Once "airborne," the runner has two choices: he can look straight ahead at second base or take a peek at the plate to see what has happened to the pitch. Morgan acknowledges that some runners can learn if and where a ball has been hit if they steal a glance at home. Thus informed, they may wish to keep running to third rather than slide or stop at second base. Morgan, however, never took his eyes off second. "The steal is a split-second play," he says. "If you're thrown out, it's usually by an eyelash. So why lose *any* time looking at the batter? If the ball is hit while you're stealing, pick up the sound of ball against bat; if it's not hit, you should be able to hear the ball hit the catcher's glove." Still, determining *where* the ball has been hit to decide whether to stop at second or head for third, may be difficult. "Look to the third-base coach for help," says Raines, who also jumps up after a successful steal to see if an errant throw might provide the opportunity to continue around the bases.

That errant throws are common enough to affect a runner's sliding style should not surprise the knowledgeable fan. The catcher, defender of last resort, has little time to steady his sights before trying to shoot a trespasser down. Watch a catcher throw to second base after the pitcher has finished between-inning warm-ups, and you will see he is almost always on target ("Right over the bag, not in the dirt, but knee high," prescribes Gold Glove second baseman Sandberg). But throw a roadrunner like Coleman into the picture and suddenly the ball has a funny way of overshooting the landing strip or coming in through the dirt.

The catcher is always fighting a clock that has begun to tick before he can do anything about it. In this battle, the runner, particularly the runner who can read pitchers, always has a head start. Catchers accept this disadvantage as a condition of their employment. "You'd like to get base stealers out at a rate of about 50 percent," says Mets' All-Star Gary Carter, "but 40 to 45 percent is more realistic. The percentage will be higher the more help the pitcher gives you."

Good catchers help the pitchers help them. "I call for the pitcher to throw to first, have him change his pattern to throw the runner off," says Carter. And good catchers help themselves. "I'll throw over to first myself," says the Cubs' Davis. "Maybe you can tire a runner out, take a step out of his legs, or at least shorten his lead."

Watch the change in a catcher's crouch when a base stealer reaches first. The throwing hand, previously tucked safely behind the thigh, emerges to tensely await its test. "On every pitch I anticipate that the runner is going," says Carter. "I'm ready to throw."

Says Davis: "When no one is on base, I'm a receiver. I try to get good and low and give a low target. I don't have to worry about blocking the ball. That all changes with a runner. You have to get into a position where you can be quick." Particularly when a left-handed batter is at the plate. The catcher can't really see the runner take off for second under those circumstances. "When a lefty is up, I have to rely on an infielder or the bench to tell me the runner is going," says Davis.

Davis is an engaging self-proclaimed country boy from Georgia whose obvious size and strength belie the fact that a strange blood disease almost killed him several seasons ago. In 1983, he provided much of the Cubs' offensive power, but his defense that season was so disappointing that the club hired Oates, a respected defensive catcher during 10 major league seasons, as special tutor. Quickness was a top priority. "Some catchers rely on arm strength, some on quickness, and some a combination of the two," says Oates. "There is a misconception that quickness means having quick hands, getting hold of the ball and getting rid of it fast. That's important. But you have to start with the feet. If your feet are slow, it doesn't matter how fast your hands are because you'll be throwing with all arm and no body strength. In football, an interior lineman needs to keep his feet under him to form a solid formation. It's the same thing when a catcher throws the ball."

Admits Davis: "If my feet don't move, I usually don't make a good throw. I'm just like the infielder who tries to throw while standing flat-footed, and I may throw it over the in-fielder's head. But if I can get my feet going, the rest of my body and my hands just seem to automatically catch up."

Now the hands do become important. "If you can grip the ball so your fingers are across the seams, you can control your throw better," says Oates. Says Carter: "Not much time to do that." Oates agrees, but still tries to get an edge by instructing his catchers to hold a ball and instinctively reach for the seams when sitting on the bench or in the clubhouse.

Oates also put Davis through special agility drills during spring training, but the breakthrough came when he pitted his catcher against the clock. "When we pretend Jody's going not against the runner, but against the stopwatch, he becomes aware of quickness and the need for footwork," says the coach. "I told him that the magic number is two seconds. In the spring of '84, he was throwing around 1.95 and 2.0, but by the middle of the season he was consistently in the 1.7s. He even had a couple in the 1.6s, fastest I've ever clocked anybody."

The results of the Davis-Oates partnership were, for the most part, encouraging. In 1983, Davis made 13 errors, allowed a league-leading 21 passed balls, and threw out only 25 percent of those trying to steal. He threw out a respectable 39 percent after Oates arrived in 1984, but then fell into his old bad habits in 1985. In 1986, he seemed to find himself again, throwing runners out at a superior rate of about 50 percent. Still, Davis had a complaint: "Oates said he'd give me $50 every time he clocked me at 1.7. I did it several times, and he only paid up once." (In 1988, Davis found himself on the bench, as rookie Damon Berryhill, an excellent defensive player, took his spot.)

Most players agree that if the catcher's throw beats the runner to second base, the umpire will usually give the defense the call unless the tag is obviously missed or late. Davis and his fellow catchers, of course, are not willing to rely on such largesse. "You're always looking for an advantage," says the backstop. "Sometimes I'll look into our opponent's dugout between pitches and watch the manager. Maybe he won't do anything for three pitches and then you see him do something a little out of the ordinary and the guy steals on that pitch. So the next time you see the same sign, maybe you pitch out."

And so the possibility of the stolen base allows ball player and fan to put on their thinking caps. Here is Willie McGee at the plate trying to figure out if he'll see a fastball because Vince Coleman is on first base; there is Roger McDowell on the mound weighing whether he should execute his best move to first base or just a deke; meanwhile, Tim Raines is at first base doing his homework and reading the pitcher. And the catcher? Poor Jody Davis, largely at his pitcher's mercy, is calculating whether he should buy precious time by letting the batter have his fastball or risk falling behind in the count by calling for the pitchout.

Doomed by his position to lose as many battles as he wins, Davis relishes the challenge when he is in the ballgame. One gets the distinct impression that the catcher does not need the promise of $50 to venture into his combat zone.

"The stolen base . . . ," says Davis. He knits his brow for a moment, then smiles the smile of a soldier happy to have the opportunity to both fire his gun and use his head. "It's one big guessing game."

6

THE MANAGER: KEEPING THE TEAM IN THE GAME

Late in the 1985 season, his team locked in a tense battle for a divisional championship, Kansas City Royals manager Dick Howser sat in the visitors' clubhouse at Comiskey Park and reflected on the previous evening's game. The Royals had lost to the Chicago White Sox in curious fashion. With two out, the bases loaded, and the score tied 1-1 in the bottom of the 9th inning, Royals' relief ace Dan Quisenberry faced Luis Salazar. Quisenberry did just what Howser had hoped for, induced Salazar to hit a routine inning-ending ground ball. But Royals' second baseman Frank White, one of the finest fielders in the game, booted the ball. By the time White recovered, Salazar was safe at first and the winning run had crossed the plate.

The loss was particularly costly. The first-place California Angels had fallen to the Yankees that evening, and the Royals, two games behind, had missed an opportunity to cut that lead in half. Despite the uncharacteristic loss, Howser was characteristically collected. He had no harsh words for White. "You don't go into a game thinking about it, but sometimes you're just not supposed to win," he said, a faint smile crossing his face. "When you throw five ground balls in an inning like Quisenberry did and get beat when a six-time Gold Glove man like White makes an error—which shows he's human—you're just not supposed to win. Look, we won the game before that one 2-1 in the 10th when our runner scored on an infield out by evading the catcher's tag."

A few hours after uttering these philosophical words, the manager tried to relax after his third 2-1 ball game in three nights. This time the Royals had beaten the White Sox when Quisenberry, in relief of Charlie Leibrandt, had stifled a 9th-inning rally by getting the dangerous Carlton Fisk to hit into a double play and Jerry Hairston to ground out to shortstop. "You're really kind of exhausted at game's end," Howser admitted. "Well, not exhausted. One guy described it as wrung out like a bar towel. You have so much going on in your mind. Coaching, you're on one level. But managing," Howser paused. "The buck stops here."

By the time the season finally ended, Dick Howser would be wrung out countless more times. The seesaw fight with the Angels for the division title was dramatic, but it pales when compared to the Royals' come-from-behind triumphs over the Toronto Blue Jays in the League Championship Series and the St. Louis Cardinals in the World Series. The Royals lasted longer on prime time than a Don Rickles sitcom, and by the time they had beaten the Cards, one of baseball's best-kept secrets was out: Since he had moved from the coaching level to managing six years earlier, Dick Howser had quietly emerged as one of the game's top managers. Sadly, less than two years after winning the Series, Howser was dead of a brain tumor.

His record was a fine one. Taking over the Yankees in 1980 after coaching third base for 10 years, Howser became only the fourth manager in history to win over 100 games in his first season. Owner George Steinbrenner rewarded the effort by firing him after the favored Yankees fell to the Royals in the League Championship Series, but the Royals liked what they had seen, and foundering in the middle of 1981, they hired Howser to replace Jim Frey. Howser promptly led the team to the second-half divisional title of that strike-shortened season. After second-place finishes the following two years, the team, despite costly injuries and even costlier revelations about the use of drugs, won the A.L. West in 1984. Then came the magic 1985 season.

Howser, who played third base for the Athletics, the Indians, and the Yankees after a distinguished collegiate career at Florida State, was the perfect choice to manage one of Middle America's most successful teams. When we talked in 1985, he told me he was aware that he lacked the flash of, say, Los Angeles' Tommy Lasorda and the volatility of Billy Martin, but he made no apology. "I don't like a lot of showmanship or flamboyant acts," he said. "With some managers it seems to be an ego thing where they try to steal the spotlight from the players. But the players really are the show."

Still, while the George Bretts, Dan Quisenberrys, and supporting Royals played on center stage in 1985, Howser could be heard if not seen. That season, in a *Sporting News* poll, his peers picked him as one of the game's three top field generals, and as much as any other manager in baseball, he was intimately involved with the front office in personnel decisions. His future seemed bright—the Royals extended his contract, and the team was the odds-on favorite to repeat in the A.L. West in 1986—but midway through the season, he was diagnosed as having a malignant brain tumor.

Because the Royals won the A.L. West in 1985 by only one game, every contest Howser managed that season was critical. Quisenberry's save of the 2-1 victory over the White Sox after his disappointing 2-1 loss kept the Royals apace with the Angels. Whether or not to bring Quisenberry in for Leibrandt was but one of the many on-the-spot decisions Howser had to make. Interestingly, he faced the same decision in two crucial World Series games as well. In Game 2 of the Series, Howser left Leibrandt in and the Cards rallied to win in the 9th. With

Kansas City facing elimination in Game 6—now memorable because of a questionable call by umpire Don Denkinger—Quisenberry eventually relieved Leibrandt and the Royals won (another 2-1 game!). Still, many observers felt Howser should have made the move to his bull pen earlier. "People are always going to second-guess you," said Howser, not the least bit troubled by that fact of life.

As second-guessing the manager is almost a national pastime in itself, knowing what a manager is thinking and doing adds one more layer to our understanding and appreciation of baseball and helps us watch a game. After the victory over the White Sox during the regular season and again after the victory in Game 6, Howser took time out to discuss with me the art of managing such games and an entire season.

Howser first explained the importance of the manager:

"I don't buy that a manager is only responsible for five or six games a year, or even 10. You can't really put your finger on how many games you're responsible for, but about half our games are decided by two runs or less. In those games, you're doing some managing!

"How do you measure that fact that your players are comfortable with you and know you're not going to lose games for them? One thing I like about baseball is that you can fool the media a little and the fans a lot, but the uniformed people can't fool each other. We're together seven days a week for seven months. We really are like a family. You know the players' strengths and weaknesses, and they know which managers can take them out of games and which can keep them in. If you do nothing more than keep your club in a ballgame, that's still managing. You're doing a helluva job."

If the Royals are playing at night, Howser's day begins at about 2 o'clock when he arrives at the ball park. When the Royals are at home, Howser's first order of business is to go over the reports phoned in each night by the Royals' minor-league managers. Then, after answering calls from the media and checking his mail, he meets with John Schuerholz, the

Royals general manager. The pair discuss happenings in and out of the Kansas City organization. "Players on other teams might be available," says Howser. "So and so in our farm system may help next year, or even the middle of next year. We're looking that far ahead."

Howser makes out his lineup early.

"As a player, I always liked to know what my role was, so as a manager, I have my lineup ready by the time the team gets to the ball park, two or three hours before the game. Some of the guys who run visitors' clubhouses around the league have told me about managers who leave a whole ashcan full of lineup cards until they settle on something. I'm not one to make a lot of lineup changes. I don't tear up too many cards.

"The ideal American League lineup would have speed guys batting number one and number two. The guy that leads off doesn't have to walk a lot, but he should get 200 hits a year. You'd rather have a left-handed hitter or a switch hitter batting second, but definitely someone who can hit to all fields. George Brett is the ideal third-place hitter—a consistent guy, a .300 hitter with power. Batters four, five, and six are power guys. Number four might put the ball in play more than the others. You want five, six, and seven to be able to break a game open late with a home run. Jim Sundberg is an excellent number-eight hitter because per at bat his r.b.i. ratio is very good even though he only hits .260 or .270. Number nine should also be a speed guy. If he can get on base with our leadoff hitter coming to the plate, a lot of things can happen.

"So you throw some speed at the other team, some power, and then some speed again. And then you go through the cycle again the next two innings. I figure if I can get my first four hitters up five times in a game, then we'll probably win."

Howser's early posting of the lineup reflects his respect for his players. Such respect, he senses, is not universal in the managerial community.

"I've heard some managers say in private that they think their players are trying to do them in. I don't believe that. It may happen occasionally, but I think it's more that players are just trying to do things in their own way. I don't know, it may be that some managers are jealous of the salaries the players are getting or that they're younger and still playing.

"I want the players to be professional, but I want them to realize baseball should be enjoyable. It's tough enough; it should be fun, too. I like them, but I don't want to get too close to them. All of a sudden you get close to a guy, and then two days later you have to send him out. You have to keep some kind of wall between yourself and the players. Ralph Houk was the epitome of a player's manager, and I was fortunate enough to work for him. He was tough personally—he had that Army training—but, if a player made a mistake, no one ever knew about it. He never jumped on any players in front of anybody else. He always closed the door first."

After making out his lineup, Howser talks with his coaches. He asks his hitting instructor which players are taking extra batting practice. There are usually four or five Royals drafted for additional time in the cage—players who haven't seen much action and players with mechanics problems.

Before beginning a new series, Howser receives an up-to-date written report on the opponent from advance scout Jerry Terrell.

"I'll meet with the pitching staff and the catchers for 15 or 20 minutes to discuss how to pitch opposing hitters. Then Mike Ferraro [third base coach in 1985] and I will go over how to defense our opponent. He handles positioning during a game, and after our talk, he'll go up to our fielders to tell them where to play particular hitters. I don't like to have the whole team in on these meetings, because everyone has an opinion, even if they've only seen another player once, and you can get bogged down.

"I enjoy numbers and spend a lot of time keeping and updating charts. I like remembering players and their strengths and weaknesses. I've been keeping my own set of charts for years, ever since I was with the Yankees."

The first page of the Royals' scouting report discusses the

other team's hot hitters. The next page lists what kind of pitches the opposing players are striking out on. This is important not so much because Howser is looking for strikeouts, but so he can see what pitches give particular hitters trouble. The next page shows what pitch pitchers use to begin a batter and how the pitching sequence goes. This helps because if, say, the Royals are facing Floyd Bannister and the White Sox just finished playing the Brewers, George Brett may ask Howser how Bannister started off against Cecil Cooper.

The following page details the situations in which the team and particular players are likely to employ certain strategies like the steal or hit and run. Terrell had done his homework for the White Sox series. His report warned that the Sox's Ozzie Guillen frequently squares around to bunt but then slaps the ball past the charging third baseman. In recent days, Guillen had victimized several teams whose scouts apparently overlooked the ploy.

Like most managers, Howser has in-house computer printouts and reports from the Elias Sports Bureau. He remains somewhat skeptical of their usefulness.

"I don't dislike the information, because it is factual. But what doesn't help me is the stuff that's 10 or 15 days old. For example, the computer might tell you that the White Sox's Floyd Bannister can really handle our Darryl Motley. But I know if Motley's swinging well, he can hit anybody. Maybe Bannister caught him on a down period. What's more important to know is which of your batters are on an upward swing and which of their pitchers are struggling. Also, if the information is based on only 10 or 15 at bats, it's not really enough to give you a true picture. So I don't do a lot of maneuvering based on the computer."

While the Royals take batting practice, Howser will generally talk on the sidelines to the media, friends, or the opposing manager. No matter how busy he is, however, he still keeps an eye on the cage.

"You can often learn more from watching a guy in batting

practice than from the computer printouts. Is the guy hitting the ball or tugging at it? How is, say, Balboni's groin problem affecting his swing?

"Fans are enamored with balls hit into the upper deck, but that's the last thing we want to see in batting practice. We want our players to practice bunting or hitting to the opposite field or maybe to get the ball on the ground more. Watch guys like Hal McRae, Jorge Orta, or Willie Wilson—they're always working on their styles of hitting."

Back in the clubhouse shortly before game time, Howser checks with his trainer to see if there are any injuries necessitating last-minute lineup changes. By now he has his game uniform on. "I have a few superstitions," he admits. "I try to wear the same shoes and sweatshirt when we win." By now, too, the butterflies have begun to dance in the manager's stomach. "About 30 minutes before a game, your nervous energy kicks in," he says. "It's different than it was as a player. As a player, you know you can work it off."

Once play begins, Howser moves around the dugout according to how the game is going.

"I want a good vantage point and a spot where our third-base coach can see me for signs. What am I watching? Everything! There's so much to think about. The other team's personnel. Our personnel. Which of our pitchers need to throw even if they're not going to get into the game. I'm also watching the positioning of our fielders. Ferraro is in charge there, but because I'm the manager, I have to stay on top of it. I rarely overrule him, but if I think a guy is out of position, I will.

"Every pitch is important. I'm not second-guessing, but I'm conscious of what our catcher is calling. I also have to keep a damn good eye on the pitcher. Is he up in the strike zone or down? Is his change-up as good as it was the last time? How about his breaking stuff? I can't see our catcher's signs, but I know our pitchers well enough so I can call every pitch. You can tell by the way the ball reacts or the hitter reacts. Maybe two or three times a game I'll ask Gary Blaylock if a pitch was a slider or a curve or if it was a change-up or a change-up off a slider.

"I don't talk very much with the players. But I don't want to be solemn. I want to have a little bit of fire, like I want the players to have. I might say, 'C'mon, let's get some runs. This pitcher's been out there long enough.' Sometimes the players—mostly Brett and McRae will ask me what a pitch was or what's in our notes about a pitcher. They might ask, say, if Seaver uses his fastball more or his change-up and if it's just a change-up or moves away from the hitter.

"Starting about the fifth inning, you have to think of all the moves you're gonna make. I have a situation in right field where I may want to beef up my defense a little bit. Occasionally, because of Lonnie Smith's throwing arm in left, I may want to get him out late in the game. My shortstops aren't hitting so I may want to pinch-hit.

"All those things. It's just constant. You never have a moment where you're not thinking about the game. Whether this guy's in the right position; whether this guy might bunt. There's a lot of talk between Ferraro and me and Blaylock and me. I'll ask Blaylock if a pitcher's stuff is good and he might say, "Yeah, but he threw 27 pitches last inning. I wouldn't go too much further with him." I won't really talk to the pitcher myself. If I have a suggestion, I'll run it through the pitching coach. In the sixth, seventh, and eighth innings, I want him to check how the guy feels. The pitcher always says he's all right, but you can tell from his tone.

"If the other team is hitting and there's nobody on base and your pitcher is breezing, or even if there's somebody on base who can't run, I'm already thinking about my lineup in the next inning. And sometimes when we're hitting and scoring runs, I'm already thinking about who the other club has coming up next inning and who they can use and who they might use if I make a move with Quisenberry."

The Royals lead 2-1, thanks to a George Brett home run. It is the top of the seventh inning. There are two out. Batting ninth, the Royals' Buddy Biancalana reaches first base when the Sox Bannister throws a wild pitch for strike three. Lonnie Smith, leading off because Wilson is injured, comes to the plate. What is Howser thinking? Should Biancalana try to steal second base?

"I want players to know that I'm in control of a ball game. You hear some television announcers that always seem to say that the runners should be started. But I'm not gonna run us out of the inning. I'm not going to do something just so people will say, 'Gee, he's an exciting manager. Look at his strategy.' "

But in this case, he does send Biancalana. Sox catcher Carlton Fisk throws him out. Howser's reasoning: "We're having trouble scoring runs. And if he's caught, Smith can lead off the next inning anyway. I know Fisk is throwing as well as he ever has, but it's a healthy gamble. If you make it, you've got your leadoff hitter with a chance to drive in a run, and if he's out,you don't have the guy in front of Brett leading the next inning."

After Leibrandt sets the Sox down in order, Lonnie Smith leads off the Royals' eighth by drawing a walk. The right-handed hitting Lynn Jones is up, with Brett on deck. Should Howser sacrifice? Hit and run? Send Smith?

"Both Wilson and Smith are safe on something like 80 percent of their stolen base attempts. That's very high. I'd rather have them steal than hit and run because they're so darn successful."

Smith steals second. In the third inning, Biancalana had bunted with a runner on second base. The sacrifice has worked, and it led to the Royals' first run. Should Jones now bunt Smith to third so that Brett can pick up the insurance run with a sacrifice fly? No. Howser lets Jones swing away and he flies out to short right field. Smith cannot advance. The manager's thoughts:

"I didn't have Jones bunt because he can go to right field so well. He knew his job. He got ahead in the count, but he just didn't hit it hard enough. I just felt like he could do it. The Sox had their first baseman on top of the hitter and their second baseman shallow. That's kind of dangerous. If you get a base hit, you've not only got a run, but a chance for a big inning. We played for a run the first time with Biancalana bunting because of the sequence of the batting order, but when I've got hitters two, three, and four in there, I'd rather not bunt. Yes, I'm already anticipating that they'll walk Brett. I've seen it so much I have to. He's so darn good."

The Sox do walk Brett intentionally, but neither Hal McRae nor Frank White can drive home the third run. The Sox then mount their own rally in the eighth. Julio Cruz leads off with a bloop hit to right, and with one out Reid Nichols chops a ball over first baseman Steve Balboni's head. The Sox have runners on first and third. The batter is Luis Salazar, who has doubled earlier. The variables Howser must weigh are mounting: he must think about his relief pitching and how to play his infield. Also, if Nichols tries to steal second, should the catcher throw through to second base? Farr is up in the Royals' bull pen, and the infield is back.

"If we tie or go behind, I'll probably use Farr. I don't like to use Quisenberry on the road unless we have a lead. Also Farr needs the work. He's done the job for us lately, and Quisenberry pitched last night. I'm thinking Nichols on first is a threat to steal, but if we throw him out, the Sox have lost the chance to score on the squeeze or sacrifice fly or even an infield out. In that situation, the catcher always checks with me whether to throw through to second base. Here, I told him to throw. We're not gonna let the winning run get to second.

"I'm playing my infield back. Yes, it's a gamble, but I'll give the Sox the tying run and try to get out of the inning. If you play the infield in and they hit the ball through that breaks the game wide open, and they have Baines and Fisk coming up. And remember, Leibrandt can get some strikeouts and the double play because he keeps the ball down."

Salazar grounds into a double play to end the eighth. In the Royals' ninth, Balboni stands at second with two out. The weak-hitting shortstop Biancalana is due up. Should Howser pinch-hit for him?

"No. Because I want his glove in the game, and I've already

got the lead. It might be different if the game were tied. If we've got a lead, I want the best defense in. Plus, the guy's been playing. If you put a new shortstop in cold, the only thing you can do is mess up." (This is exactly what happened when Howser substituted Onix Concepcion for Biancalana in the 10th inning of the second game of the League Championship Series. Concepcion's failure to make a routine play contributed to the Blue Jays' come-from-behind victory.)

Howser seems to be pushing all the right buttons now. Biancalana singles, and Balboni stops at third. But, Smith can't drive him in. In the Sox's ninth, Harold Baines leads off with a single, but Quisenberry comes in to put out the fire. Will the victory give the Royals momentum?

"I really don't believe in momentum in baseball. 'Momentum' is good pitching every day. It's winning 12 out of 16 games or 18 out of 25. You can't have a football mentality—thinking about an unbeaten season or winning 20 in a row. You better be prepared to grind it out, because there are games when you're playing well and you're still gonna get beat 2-1. People will say, 'That's a tough loss.' But what loss isn't tough? You're paid to win. Fans are more emotional about games than a manager, because they can afford to be. They believe more in momentum and moves and strategy, whereas the manager understands you can only do so much. You better be prepared. You better not let the other guy make a move you're not aware of, but you also better understand there are days you're just not gonna win. If you manage long enough, you have certain games where you do everything you think is right and it just doesn't work out. You send in a defensive replacement and he loses it in the lights . . . ."

Now let us move to Game 6 of the 1985 World Series. You may remember the circumstances: the Royals trail the Cardinals three games to two in the best-of-seven showdown. After three games in St. Louis, the Series has moved back to Kansas City for its conclusion. Leibrandt is on the mound for the Royals. He has been superb in postseason play. He faces Danny Cox, who won 18 games during the regular season for the Cards. The two pitched in Game 2, which the Cardinals won 4-2 when they scored four runs in the ninth inning. In some quarters, Howser, much more visible now because the television camera focuses on him constantly, was severely criticized for failing to replace Leibrandt with Quisenberry.

Pitching has dominated the Series to date; each team is having trouble scoring runs. If the Royals can win and force a seventh and deciding game, another pitchers' duel is likely. The Royals' best pitcher, Bret Saberhagen, would face the Cardinals' ace, John Tudor. Despite being down 3-2, Howser is confident. "We're back in Kansas City and we have our two best pitchers ready for the last two games. I'd overheard a St. Louis player say he didn't want to have to go back to Kansas City. I knew the reason. It wasn't Dick Howser and it wasn't the ball park; it was who we had pitching."

Having already learned how Howser manages a regular season contest, let's watch (and manage along with) him here:

Is the preparation for such a game different?

"Not really. Even though we haven't been hitting and Cox pitched well against us in Game 2, I'm not going to make any lineup changes. That time of the year you don't want to get too fancy.

"There is one difference—what you do in your bull pen. Because the whole bull pen is rested. You're really set up well in that regard. It's not like during the season where you might not be able to use a guy for a day or two because he's tired."

Although Leibrandt has been outstanding, the Royals have not been scoring runs for him and he has not been rewarded with a victory. One might think a special pep talk from the manager is in order before taking the mound.

"No. Anyone who wins 17 games during the regular season doesn't need a lift. Knowing Charlie, he's confident. He's beaten a lot of good clubs. He's pitching his good stuff and knows he can beat anybody. We didn't even go over the

Cardinals' hitters before the game. We'd done that at the beginning of the Series."

The first inning.   The Cardinals go down in order. Lonnie Smith, inserted in the leadoff spot in front of Willie Wilson during the playoffs, starts the Royals off with a double. Should the speedy Smith try to make something happen by stealing third? The Royals haven't been scoring, and it would be nice if Leibrandt had a lead for one of the few times in postseason play. Smith has the green light from Howser to steal third base whenever he wants. Such faith results from, among other things, Howser's viewing of the Cardinals on television much earlier in the year. Smith, who was then with St. Louis, stole third so easily that when the Royals traded for him later in the season, Howser said, in effect, "Steal when you want to."

"Lonnie does have the green light, but if everything isn't perfect, you don't want him to steal here. He had stolen third earlier in the Series when a left-handed hitter was up [more difficult because the catcher has a better view and a better lane to throw], so you're always looking for it to happen, but so is the other club. Particularly the Cards because they played with him, know him well. With nobody out, I'd rather he wait. Getting thrown out at third isn't like getting thrown out at second with nobody out."

But wouldn't an early lead be a boost for the hard-luck Leibrandt?

"Getting a one-run lead that early doesn't really mean anything. It's not going to change the Cards' strategy. They're still going to run. They're gonna run if they're four or five runs down. The only thing they may not do is hit and run. But they steal more than they hit and run anyway. People think, 'Boy, you get a one-run lead.' But those leads don't hold. You may win 1-0, but it doesn't change the other team's approach. And it doesn't change your pitcher's approach. The good pitcher's don't change a whole lot even if they have a five- or six-run lead. They still have to pitch their pattern. Especially Charlie. His style never changes."

If Smith does reach third, there is always the possibility that the Cardinals might walk Brett, who is, as usual, carrying the Royals' offense. On the bench, Howser wonders about this.

"I don't know what they're going to do. But I'd say that that early in the game, I would doubt it. You start putting on runners early, and now instead of a one-run game, you've got a chance of being two or three runs down. What that does to your club is make them say, 'What the hell are we doing?' To me that's not good baseball. And if you don't do it during the regular season, why do it during the World Series?"

Smith does not steal, and the Royals do not score. In this inning (and again later in the game), home plate umpire Jim Quick angers a few Royals batters by calling strikes on some pitches that may have been balls. In the dugout, Howser looks annoyed.

"I'd rather not comment on the umpiring. Anytime you're in a playoff or World Series, the calls are more critical. But I'd never fault the umpire, because there's as much pressure on him as on the players. I admit I'm probably a little more cranked up. There's more at stake. But it's not like you go into the game and say, 'I'm gonna get on the umpires more.' You're just at a higher stress point."

The second inning.   Three up, three down for the Cards. The Royals get a hit, but do not score.

The third inning.   Leibrandt sets the Cards down in order for the third inning in a row. Can Howser sense whether Leibrandt has his good stuff?

"I'm not good enough to tell. Some people say they can tell after the first inning. I don't believe that. Things change too quickly in this game. That's why a manager never has a chance to feel real good about things. Even in Game 7 (which the Royals won 11-0), I didn't feel real good until we had a seven or eight-run lead. The delay situation [occasioned by the ejections of St. Louis pitcher Joaquin Andujar and manager Whitey Herzog] bothered the heck out of me. I'm not faulting Andujar or the Cards, but it's like a rain delay. When you have a big lead, the only thing it can do is work against you."

Leibrandt strikes out to lead off the Royals' half of the inning. Much was made of the fact that Howser might be at a disadvantage managing in the Series because his pitchers would have to bat (unlike the regular season, during which American League teams use a designated hitter to bat for the pitcher). The designated-hitter rule does eliminate a certain amount of strategizing because it eliminates the issue of whether to pinch-hit for the pitcher. When National League managers pinch-hit for the pitcher, they often "flip-flop" a player in the next inning. That is, they replace a player in the next inning as well as the pitcher, but switch their replacements in the batting order, so that the player now hitting in the previous pitcher's spot in the order, will bat before the new pitcher does.

"Was that a big deal? The writers made it a big deal, didn't they? Listen, we flip-flopped in one game and still got beat. Without being overconfident, let me say that managers can adjust. It's not that big a deal. I'm not used to doing it. I'm a little uncomfortable because I haven't done it a lot. But I didn't feel any extra pressure to either take a guy out or leave him in. Maybe it was the way the Series went, but I didn't lie awake at night worrying about flip-flopping my pitcher and right fielder or when I was gonna take a guy out for a pinch hitter."

The fourth inning.   The game is still scoreless. The Cards again fail to get a base runner; Leibrandt has retired the first 12 men he has faced. With one out, Frank White surprises the Cardinals by bunting for a hit, but is thrown out stealing. How much did the manager have to do with this chain of events?

"I have a sign I sometimes give that means 'bunt for a base hit.' But in this game, White did it on his own. He's very good at that.

"I did give the steal sign here. I was just trying to get

runners in scoring positions. Frank is a pretty good runner. He didn't get a good lead, but if you watch him, he rarely does. He depends more on lulling the pitcher to sleep."

The Royals' next hitter, Pat Sheridan, singles. Now, many fans are second-guessing Howser. If White had not tried to steal, he would be sitting on third base and the Royals, with one less out, would have a better chance to score.

"I don't understand that reasoning. Sheridan would not have gotten the same pitch to hit. The pitch selection changes with a guy on first or second or a guy up with nobody on base. Nothing is the same. Location is never the same. So I always get a kick out of it after a guy hits a home run and someone says, 'If you hadn't stolen, you'd have two runs.'

"See what I'm saying? The catcher mixes everything up. Rarely will two balls be thrown in the same area, the same pitch, more than every three or four innings. People reason like that, but it just isn't so. Otherwise, you'd be much more reluctant to steal or hit and run."

The fifth inning.   Leibrandt remains perfect. Sundberg leads off the Royals' half of the inning with a single. Biancalana, a weak hitter all season, is doing well at the plate in the Series. Should he sacrifice bunt with the even-weaker-hitting pitcher following him in the order? Howser says no.

"Yes, the fact that Leibrandt is coming up makes a helluva difference. The reason that Biancalana had such a good Series—and his on-base percentage was even more impressive than his batting average—was that for the first time all year, they were pitching around him to get to the pitcher. They do that in the National League; they can pitch around more people knowing the pitcher has to hit.

"I didn't have Biancalana sacrifice because even if he was successful, I'd have only had one real shot at getting Sundberg home [because Leibrandt would, presumably, have been an easy out]. And if you're not successful with the sacrifice, you've screwed up your lineup, because now you've got a man on first, one out, and the pitcher up."

Biancalana flies out, creating the same effect as if he had

missed the sacrifice: man on first, one out, Leibrandt up. Leibrandt successfully executes a sacrifice bunt. "You bunt because you don't want your pitcher hitting into a double-play," explains Howser.

Smith makes the third out. Through five innings there is no score. The Royals have had a few opportunities, but the Cardinals have yet to have a base runner. If you are Howser are you confident?

"No, I'm not confident! I feel good about the way the game is going, but I'm not confident. As a manager, I want to either have a lead or be close. What's close? Two or three runs is still close. The only thing that I liked was that we were at home and we were in the game.

"The fact that we weren't hitting very well didn't bother me because I've seen so much of that with this ball club. You have to be philosophical. If you're not going to hit .280 as a team, you're not going to hit .280. The thing that did surprise me was the next night when we scored 11 runs.

"But this game was going as you'd expect when you've got Leibrandt pitching and they have their number-two pitcher."

The sixth inning.   Cesar Cedeno leads off the inning for the Cardinals with their first base hit. The ball falls in front of left fielder Smith, who appeared to have a chance to catch it if he had gambled and charged it. The next batter, Darrell Porter, also singles and Cedeno moves to second. Should Howser phone his bull pen?

"There's no real reason to get anybody up in the bull pen. Their pitcher is up next. But also, even if those two runs score, Charlie's still pitching a good ball game."

Predictably, Cox bunts. Howser has put on the "rotation play" to defend against this. That is, instead of moving to cover second base while the second baseman covers first, shortstop Biancalana moves to cover third base for the possible force out there. Former Yankee manager Billy Martin and others in the American League use the rotation play frequently, but Howser does not.

"You can use it like I did against the Cards, because in the National League you know the pitcher is going to bunt. But use that play too often in the American League and the ninth-place hitter won't bunt but instead will hit and run on you [the hitter will try to put the ball into that wide area vacated by the shortstop who has moved to third base]. Then you're in deep trouble."

This time the play works. Cox pops a bunt to charging third baseman Brett. It appears that Brett could have intentionally dropped the ball, then started a double play. On the bench, is Howser bothered by Brett's decision to catch the ball or Smith's earlier decision not to charge?

"I'm not the left fielder; I'd rather Smith use his own judgment. I know on an artificial surface the way the ball bounces that if you let that ball get by you, you're probably giving them a run. The one thing you don't want in that situation is to give them a double or triple to lead off the inning. Lonnie is a good enough player to understand that. Would I talk to him on the bench if I thought he should have caught it? No. I rarely talk about that kind of thing, and if I did it would be the next day. You work on those things in practice.

"As for George's decision, he did the right thing. You want the out there. What happens if you drop the ball on purpose and then don't get anybody out? We talk to our players about that. You don't want to get too fancy. You want to get the lead runner out; then you can go for the double play."

Howser's conservatism pays off. The next batter, Ozzie Smith, ends the Cards' threat by grounding into a double play. Willie Wilson leads off the Royals' sixth with a single. Brett is up. Is Wilson, who has the green light, less likely to steal knowing that if he's successful, the Cardinals might intentionally walk Brett?

"Not really. Not when he's started off the inning with a hit. I don't think they'll walk Brett with nobody out. But what Wilson will do is give George at least one chance to swing at the ball rather than run right away."

Brett grounds into a double play. The man who has been

shouldering most of the Royals' offense is now 0 for 3, having also struck out and flied to right field. Is Howser worried that his big gun is silent tonight?

"I know the fans worry, but I don't. He can't do it all the time. People get conned into thinking George is going to do it every time or that Quisenberry is going to get batters out all the time. No, if George has made three outs in a game, I feel good about his next at bat. I want him to get up again. If the game stays like it is, he'll get another at bat and that will be the critical one."

The seventh inning.   The score is still 0-0. Leibrandt sets the Cards down in order. The Royals mount a threat. Sheridan strikes out, but Balboni walks. Anticipating that he may want to pinch-hit for Leibrandt, Howser has Quisenberry warming up in the bull pen. Sundberg strikes out, but Biancalana singles. Balboni stops at second base.

Howser has a tough decision to make. With two outs and runners on first and second should he pinch-hit for Leibrandt? Howser knows Leibrandt is almost certain to end the inning if he bats. But he is pitching a sensational game. This is a decision the manager would not have to make in the American League because of the designated hitter rule. Remember, Howser stuck with Leibrandt in Game 2 (a little too long, according to his critics) and the Cards eventually won. Leibrandt bats for himself and strikes out. In the stands and in the broadcast booth, the second-guessers are having a field day.

"I left Charlie in because he was still pitching a good game. There are two ways to think about it: if you pinch-hit for him and get a hit, it's a good move. If you don't get a hit and the relief pitcher comes in and gets beat, it's not a good move. The way Leibrandt was pitching, I wanted to see him in the ball game. I don't think anybody could have pitched better than he did. Now, if we'd had men in real scoring position, on third base with less than two outs where all we needed was a fly ball or ground out, yeah, then I would have hit for him.

"Would I have made the same move in the 8th or 9th inning? I can't say. We don't know. I'd have to get a feel for what was going on. I don't think you can say what you'd do. I don't think you can manage that way."

The eighth inning. The Cards' Tito Landrum flies to center. Terry Pendleton follows with a single. Leibrandt then issues his first walk to Cedeno. There is activity in the Royals' bull pen.

"Once they start getting runners on late in the game, somebody's up in the bull pen."

Howser has one eye on this half of the inning and one eye on the Royals' half. "I'm thinking ahead. We've got the top of our order coming up. I just want some runners on base because I've seen so many things that those guys at the top of our order can do."

Leibrandt strikes out Porter, then gets two quick strikes on Brian Harper, who is pinch-hitting for Cox. A ball. And then Harper hits a little looper that falls for a hit in short center field. The Cardinals score the first run of the game. Does Howser's heart sink with those of the Kansas City fans?

"Not really. Leibrandt was still pitching well. The hit was off the end of the bat. Guys are gonna get hits; that's what they're paid for. When someone dumps one in like that, there's nothing you can do. It was still just a one-run game, and being at home, we had the final say-so."

Leibrandt walks the next batter, Ozzie Smith. Howser calls for Quisenberry: "I just felt it was time for a change."

Quisenberry retires Willie McGee to end the inning. Ken Dayley, a left-hander, replaces the right-handed Cox on the mound. This forces Howser to reconsider how he might use pinch hitters if the need arises. He would rather have had a left-handed hitter facing Cox, but will now want a right-handed pinch hitter to face Dayley. With one out Wilson singles. Should he try to steal second so Brett can drive him home with a single? He doesn't go. Brett strikes out, and White flies out to end the inning.

"Dayley is a lefty and has a good move to first base. Wilson probably couldn't read it that well. Yes, Wilson's usually on his own, but I might not want him to run in this situation. I don't want him to get thrown out or picked off with Brett hitting. Brett is one of the total-base leaders in baseball. He can score Willie from first base on a long single in our park. Of course, I'd prefer if Wilson's on second base, but you have to think about pitchouts, throws to first base. There are a lot of things to be considered."

The ninth inning.   The Cardinals fail to score. Trailing 1-0, the Royals must register a run or St. Louis will be World Champions. Howser has spent the top of the inning figuring out how he will use his bench.

First move: he sends up the right-handed Darryl Motley to pinch-hit for the left-handed Pat Sheridan. Herzog counters by bringing in the right-handed fastball pitcher Todd Worrell.

Second move: Howser replaces Motley before he reaches the plate with Jorge Orta.("I want an experienced left-handed batter to face Worrell.")

Orta triggers one of the most controversial plays in recent World Series history by hitting a slow dribbler down the first-base line. First baseman Jack Clark fields it and throws to Worrell, who has run to cover first base. Worrell appears to beat Orta. But the umpire calls Orta safe. Herzog argues vehemently, but the call stands. (Replays show Orta was indeed out.)

"It was not a routine play, and it looked a helluva lot closer in the park than it did on the replay. No, I didn't worry about the umpire changing the call. I've never seen that happen unless interference or some type of obstruction is called."

After Clark drops a popup in foul territory, Balboni singles. Orta stops at second base.

Third move: Howser sends the fleet Onix Concepcion to run for the slower Balboni: "He represents the winning run. I gotta get some legs in there."

But what if the Royals only tie the game? Won't they miss

Balboni's bat in extra innings? "I don't have the luxury of worrying about that."

Fourth move: Howser orders Sundberg to sacrifice the runners into scoring position. Sundberg fails, forcing Orta at third. Runners remain at first and second with one out.

Fifth move: Howser sends his best hitter on the bench, Hal McRae, to pinch-hit for Biancalana.

"I use McRae before anybody else here because he's our best r.b.i. man. I don't want him sitting on the bench next to me with the game over, never having been used. I have a lot of confidence in Dane Iorg, who's also on the bench, but the second half of the season, McRae was our big r.b.i. man."

A passed ball moves the runners to second and third, forcing Worrell to intentionally walk McRae.

Sixth move: Howser sends Iorg to pinch-hit for Quisenberry. Any last-minute instructions?

"I can't tell him anything he doesn't already know. Dane used to be with St. Louis, so he knows Worrell, knows he'll be challenged with a fastball."

Iorg singles to right.

"When he hit it, I knew we'd get one run; I didn't know if Sundberg would score from second base, too.

"Yes, I'm already thinking about the next inning (if it's a tie game). Who's gonna pitch? Concepcion can replace Biancalana; Iorg can replace Sheridan; and Jamie Quirk can replace Balboni at first. Actually, you've got to think about those things before the inning even starts. I'm thinking there are two things that can happen. If we win, I don't have to worry about the tenth. But we might tie, so you have to be prepared."

Sundberg does score. The Royals win, forcing a seventh game. How soon before Howser starts worrying about tomorrow?

"You want to enjoy this game before worrying about Game 7. I knew we had Saberhagen pitching. And if we can't beat 'em with Leibrandt and Saberhagen, we're not gonna beat 'em."

It was not by chance that Howser had his two best pitchers ready for the last two games. He had planned his rotation that way (just as Herzog, thought by many to be the top manager in the game, had his two aces lined up). How much does managing come into play in the World Series?

"I think when it comes down to the World Series it matters a lot. There are a lot of critical decisions to make. One thing is for sure. People are going to second-guess you whatever decision you make. I've lived through that. I can handle that. As manager I try to do the best job I can do. I don't second-guess myself.

"Some announcers and fans want you to do more. But you are doing a lot more than people give you credit for. No one will ever know until they're down here doing it. Some people think just because I'm not animated, I'm not doing anything. But that's not my style."

Howser said it took him several days to recover from the World Series.

"There are times when managing is tough—when you don't sleep well, when you have a nervous stomach, when things are awfully uptight. I really feel for managers whose teams are 30 games under .500. I don't know if I could do that. But there's a lot of satisfaction in managing, and as bad as things sometimes get, it's a helluva way to make a living. I look forward to all the pressures of being in the World Series again real soon."

Postscript: Dick Howser's untimely death in 1986 shocked and saddened everyone in the baseball world. Ironically, when selecting a manager for this chapter—it was the middle of the 1985 season—I did not choose Howser because I thought the Royals would soon be world champions. Managers don't always last long in town, and I was looking for someone who would more than likely be holding down the same job when the book came out. I had also heard Howser was among the game's most accessible managers. He was more than accessible. He gave me all the time I wanted.

He was pleasant, engaging and forthright. And he was a study in class. (After an article I wrote about him appeared in January 1986, he called to thank me.) It was obvious during our several hours together that he relished talking—not about himself—but about the game he so dearly loved. He is sorely missed, both on and off the field.

7
ON-FIELD COMMUNICATION: CRIES AND WHISPERS

The late Dick Howser once recalled a confrontation with umpire Nick Bremigan. "A few years ago in Seattle we had some trouble with Nick and his crew. I respect Nick, but there were two plays where I thought Seattle's first baseman was way off the bag. The second time I went out to argue, I knew I was gonna be thrown out. So I got on Nick about his hairpiece. I told him he ought to take his dime-store wig and shove it up his you know what. And he threw me out. But the thing I liked about it was that the next day at home plate he brought me a cheap hairpiece. He'd gone out and bought one! He said, 'Dick, I know what you told me to do with the other one.' I thought that was good. I told him that was the way umpires should approach the game. Last night is history."

Would that we fans could become historians and eavesdrop on all the conversations that take place during the course of a baseball game. The dialogue between manager and umpire, catcher and umpire, batter and umpire, batter and catcher, coach and pitcher, pitcher and catcher, infielder and base runner. The chatter on the bench, the levity in the bull pen. What are they saying?

Would, too, that we could understand those elaborate gyrations of the third-base coach, become readers of the special language that is telegraphed from manager to coach and then to batter and base runner. And what about the signs a catcher sends to his pitcher to call for a fastball, curve, slider, or change-up? What are they "saying" out there?

There is no shortage of stories in the baseball world about the spirited tête-à-têtes between umpires and managers or players who feel they have been wronged. The Los Angeles Dodgers' colorful manager Tommy Lasorda recalls the time he ran onto the field to protest a call by the late umpire Lee Weyer: "I started after him to tell him he missed the play, and he started telling me, 'What time you gonna be at that restaurant, Tommy?' And I said, 'Well, I'll be there at 7 o'clock. But, Lee, you missed the play.' And he said, 'Is the food still good down there, Tommy?' Well, we went through the whole thing. Yet he got his point across and I got mine."

In a game of inches—in which split-second judgments must be made about the precise location of a baseball whizzing by at 90 miles an hour or whether, amid a tangle of spikes and knees and dust, a fielder tagged a runner before the runner tagged the base—there are bound to be disagreements. In a game that is so physical, those disagreements are bound, at times, to become heated. But rare is the ball player or manager who doesn't, in the abstract at least, feel for the umpire. Even rarer is the player who would want the ump's job. Says Walt Terrell, the Detroit Tigers' fine starting pitcher, "I've never won 35 games in a season, and I don't think any umpire has ever called 35 straight great games. But they do the best they can. I wouldn't want the job. I don't know too many people who would."

The umpire most likely to be in the hot seat is the man behind the plate, who must determine whether a ball coming in head on at lethal speed or curving or sliding or knuckling at the last second is in that amorphous area known as the strike zone. The rules of baseball mandate that if a manager, coach, or player argues over a ball or a strike, he is subject to automatic ejection (just as he is if he gives the ump the "choke" sign or throws equipment at him). But discussion is not only allowed, it is commonplace. Says veteran National League umpire John Kibler, "A lot of times after a batter swings at a pitch and misses, he'll ask if it was a strike. And if it's a called strike, he might ask if it caught the whole plate or just the corner." Kibler and his brethren are more than happy to handle such queries, particularly if they are just informational.

As might be expected, however, the discussions often go beyond the "just asking" stage. Catcher, batter, or pitcher might register displeasure with the verdict. If you see a catcher keep his glove where he caught the pitch just a little bit longer before throwing it back to the mound, if you see a batter shake his head and step out of the batter's box, if you see a pitcher turn his back to the plate and walk off the mound, odds are he feels he has been wronged. There is a protocol here—a right way and wrong way to behave or speak. Reggie Jackson explains the etiquette: "If you want to question a pitch, you do it subtly. You might look down at the ground, rub your nose, put your hand over your mouth, then say, 'That ball was a little high wasn't it?' Or 'I thought the ball was low.' "

Catchers, who must live and die with the umpire's decisions all day long, have to be even more diplomatic than batters. "There's a right way and wrong way to handle a missed pitch," says the Dodgers' Mike Scioscia. "First, I like to ask an umpire where the pitch was, if he thought it was low, for example. That way I can get an idea of the strike zone he's using. Then, if there's any disagreement I can voice my opinion, say, 'I didn't think that was low.' The one thing you don't want to do is turn around. If you turn around and yell, particularly if you're at home, the hostility can build in the stands and you're going to bring undue attention on the umpire."

If a player treats an umpire in a professional way, he will probably get a professional reply. "If it was a close pitch that could have gone either way, I'll say, 'Tough call, tough call,'" says Kibler.

Says Scioscia, "Most umpires will talk to you and either admit they were wrong (although they won't change the call) or say it's their judgment and that's the end of the argument. Umpires realize they're human and are gonna make mistakes. If an ump has a bad day, he may be in a slump just like a hitter is. Usually if he misses a pitch, he'll just flat out say, 'I missed it.' "

Since the dialogue between pitcher and umpire must be carried on from a distance of over 60 feet, a form of nonverbal communication has emerged. "If it's a close pitch, you might give the umpire a little signal from the mound," says the New York Yankees' Ron Guidry. Guidry moves his hand back and forth, then above his chest. "Was it away? Was it up? A lot of times the umpire won't say anything back. He'll just look at you and make a sign." Guidry pauses and makes a motion like a parking lot attendant directing someone into a narrow space. "That means he missed it. Okay, no problem. That means you can throw the pitch in the same spot again and he'll call it a strike."

A pitcher and umpire may have the opportunity to talk after an inning. "You might be running back to the dugout and ask, 'Hey, where were those two pitches to the last guy?'" says Guidry. "He might answer, 'They were close. I could have missed them.' He'll let you know, if he's a good umpire. Or he'll say, 'Well, I'm having a little trouble, bear with me.' Umpires are trying to do the best job they can. If they're having trouble and you don't get on them, they get better for you. They give you some pitches. They try to call a better game, because you're trying to battle your butt off and they know it's their fault if they're hurting you, they'll try harder."

Guidry's attitude has put him in good stead with the American League umpires. While no one will acknowledge that showing up an umpire will result in an intentional effort on the ump's part to miss a call, few players want to get on the bad side of the man calling balls and strikes. Says Brett, "It's good to have umpires on your side, and I try to keep them on mine. It's not gonna hurt. I don't want any umpire to hold a grudge against me."

As long as a player or manager behaves civilly to an umpire, he will not start a civil war. How far can he go without disturbing the peace? Says Kibler, "No one likes to be yelled at in front of a ball park full of people. A lot of times a manager will come out and say, 'I'm just out to protect my player. I don't want you to run him.' That's fine. Beyond that, different people have different temperaments, but no good umpire is going to let anyone attack him personally. If someone calls you a name, you'll eject him. If someone argues and argues and won't leave, I finally say, 'You've been here long enough, if you don't leave now, I'll have to throw you out.' Then if he says, 'Well, I'm not leaving,' I don't have any choice."

The managers and players know how far they can go. Says Lasorda, "You can discuss your point. They'll even allow you to tell them they were wrong. But the thing they won't stand for is profanity or saying something personal about their family."

Jackson gets down to the nitty-gritty. "They won't usually throw you out if you've got a legitimate gripe as long as you don't prolong it. But profanity directed personally at the umpire can get you thrown out. You can say, 'That damn ball was low.' Or, 'That was a horse—— call.' They'll take that kind of thing. But you can't say, 'You're an s.o.b.' Or, 'Go to hell.' Or, 'You're f—— crazy.' "

And what if you do cross the line? "Once you're gone, get your money's worth," says the Yankees' Dave Winfield, smiling.

Not all the talk at home plate centers on the umpire's calls.

There is a good deal of friendly banter that goes on between umpire, batter, and catcher. Says Brett: "When I get up to the plate the first time, I'll tell a guy he's my favorite umpire. Like with Ken Keyser: 'Hey, you're my favorite.' Then he'll look at the third-base ump, who'll look at the second-base ump, who'll look to first base, and they'll all kind of give a funny shrug. I just try to have fun up there."

Adds Jackson, "If you've been around, you'll talk to an umpire, particularly when, say, the catcher is out talking to the pitcher. You'll just ask how his family is, stuff like that."

When Jackson was batting, his chatter with a catcher was along the same lines. "It's not much more than 'Hello' unless you've played with a guy for a long time. Like, [former Orioles' catcher] Rick Dempsey and I were teammates in Baltimore, so I might say, 'How ya doing? How was your winter? Looks like you're swinging the bat pretty well. Good luck to you, buddy. Good to see you.'"

Sometimes the conversation is "shop talk," a discussion of a particular play in the game, of the season in general, or the talents of the man on the mound. The Cubs' Jody Davis recalls a talk with Mets' catcher Gary Carter: "I kept telling him, 'Boy that [Mets' relief pitcher] Roger McDowell throws a wicked slider.'" Similar conversations take place between infielders and base runners. When Don Mattingly is playing first base for the Yankees, he'll ask the man who just singled how the pitcher pitched him or if he was looking for a particular pitch.

Most catchers are as professional with batters as they are with umpires. "It's a far cry from Little League," says Scioscia. "There's not the 'Hey, batter batter' you might think. That stuff doesn't go over too well in the big leagues." Still, some catchers—the Cardinals' Tony Pena, for example—are real chatterboxes. As hitting requires a great deal of concentration, some batters don't like to be bothered by such chatter. There is a certain amount of gamesmanship here. The late Thurman Munson, a standout catcher with the Yankees in the 1970s, was a master at distracting hitters. Says former Royals' designated hitter Hal McRae, "I don't talk at all at the plate, and I don't like for the catcher to talk to me. Generally most guys respect your wishes. But Munson talked constantly. There were times when I would tell the umpire to make him shut up. He intentionally talked. He'd tell you how tired he was, how he wasn't swinging the bat well, how he couldn't wait for the season to end, just to get your mind off of what you were doing at the plate."

Will an umpire oblige a batter and silence the tormentor? "Yes," says Kibler, "but I can only recall doing it twice in my 22 years. You just tap the catcher on the shoulder and say, 'That's enough.' Then everyone laughs and it's over."

If there is an effort to distract a player on the field, it may come from the opposing bench. Tigers' pitcher Frank Tanana, who has gone from being a fastball-oriented power pitcher to a finesse pitcher with a variety of off-speed offerings, says he is sometimes the target of slings and arrows. "I'll hear them say, why don't you stop throwing that junk and throw a fastball," he says, smiling. Does it bother him? "Not really. It shows I have them frustrated."

Despite Tanana's experience, bench jockeying, as the art of riding an opponent is called, is in danger of becoming a lost art. Says the fiery Cubs' manager Don Zimmer, "Years ago there were certain managers that loved to hear a couple of their players get on a visiting pitcher or something, but it doesn't happen too much today."

Zimmer does, however, remember one incident from 1986, when he was the Yankees' third base coach. "The Tigers' Kirk Gibson hit a real shot, but our first baseman caught it and turned it into a double play. Gibson was frustrated, and when he got back to his dugout, he was hollering at our pitcher, 'You lucky so and so.' Then our catcher Ron Hassey looked at him, and Gibson said something to him. Hassey got hot and started over to the Tigers' bench. But Gibson, who I've been told by many people is a very rough, tough guy, never moved off his seat. The next time he came to the plate he apologized to Hassey, and said, 'That wasn't right of me.'"

Most conversation on the bench is directed not to the opposition but to teammates. Says the Royals' Frank White, "You never take it easy in the dugout. Most of the time you're watching the pitcher or talking to someone about your last at bat. Hal McRae and I would talk a lot about hitting. You're constantly talking baseball." Adds teammate Brett, "The first time I face a guy, I may come back to the dugout and say, 'Hey, his fastball is really running away.' Or, 'He's got a good change-up.' "

As Reggie Jackson neared the end of his career, he found himself playing three different roles. He was primarily a designated hitter, but sometimes he played right field, and sometimes he was on the bench waiting to be used as a pinch hitter. Here are his insights into being in the dugout in these varying capacities:

"If you're playing in the field on a given day, you're automatically in the game when you sit on the bench. Your heart is beating faster, your blood is running faster. You're involved in the game emotionally, mentally, meaning how is the guy throwing, what's he getting over for balls and strikes, how you're swinging the bat.

"If you're the designated hitter, you follow the game and stay alert. You're emotionally involved, but not quite as much as a guy who's playing in the field. But you have to be ready. You can't all of a sudden turn it on and get ready to hit.

"If you're not playing at all, but know you may pinch-hit, you can relax for two or three innings. But after you relax, your body will be stiff. You'll be uncomfortable. Your muscles won't be ready to fire immediately if the manager calls on you to go into the game. So you'll see a lot of players that sit in one spot on the bench for an inning or two, but then they'll get up. They'll walk into the clubhouse, get up and get a drink of water, pat somebody on the back, anticipate something by yelling because they need to stay involved. That way it will take less for them to get ready if they're needed. You'll walk around the dugout, maybe run out and catch a few balls with the outfielders between innings, bring somebody their glove, pick up a guy's helmet, anything so that you're not just sprawled out on the bench daydreaming."

When a designated hitter's at bat approaches or a pinch hitter anticipates a trip to the plate, he will generally leave the dugout and go to the clubhouse to stretch and swing the bat. (There, he may run into the club's stopper—the relief pitcher used in crucial late-inning situations. Minnesota's Jeff Reardon, for example, goes into the trainer's room with the assistant trainer around the third inning to get stretched.) Manny Mota, one of the game's great pinch hitters and now a coach with the Dodgers, would spend the early innings of a game in a batting cage under the stands to prepare himself for pinch-hitting chores. When he was on the bench, Mota tried to think of ways to help the club. "You can watch the pitcher, maybe pick something up, and give it to the rest of the guys," says Mota. Adds the Tigers' reserve outfielder John Grubb, "The guys on the bench are always looking to help. Sometimes we'll see that a pitcher is tipping a pitch. Sometimes we may be able to steal a sign."

While the reserve hitters sit on the bench during the game, the relief pitchers sit in the bull pen. What goes on there? "It's very loose for the first few innings," says Vern Hoscheit, the coach who once ran the Mets' bull pen. "We have a television set out there, so we can watch the game, see replays. Some of the fans tease us and ask what shows we're watching, but it's always on the game. Guys shoot sunflower seeds at each other, find a stick to play hockey, or dig holes in the dirt and play golf. But after the fifth inning it gets serious. And when the phone rings everyone is all business. The guys are like racehorses. When the bell sounds they're ready."

Hoscheit would bring a chart to the bull pen that listed the tendencies of all the hitters on the opposing club. "Let's say there is early trouble and the other club has a lot of lefties in their lineup. Then our lefty, who would probably go in, will be studying the charts."

Hoscheit has been in bull pens from Oakland to Baltimore to New York. Who was the merriest prankster? "Baltimore's Moe Drabowsky," he says. "He'd do things like light a whole series of firecrackers with real slow fuses under the bull pen bench. The guys would be sitting there and then all of a sudden there'd be a bang. Then a little later another bang and another." But Drabowsky's greatest trick was reserved for the opposition. Remembers Hoscheit, "In those days you could call anywhere you wanted to on the bull pen phone. Well, Moe would pretend he was a coach and call the visiting team's bull pen and tell them to get so and so up. And they'd do it."

Before a relief pitcher enters a game, it is more than likely that the manager or pitching coach or catcher or all three will have talked to the pitcher struggling on the mound. What do they talk about during such conferences? Says Lasorda, "There are different conversations depending on the situation in the game. Sometimes I go out and pat 'em on the butt. Sometimes I don't say anything. And sometimes I chew 'em out. That's when they're not concentrating, not doing the job like I think they should be doing it."

Scioscia's discussions are equally varied. "It depends on the pitcher," he says. "I might say something off the wall, like, 'Where did you eat last night?' just to break a bad train of thought. Or I may have to chew him out, tell him to get his stuff together. This is where a catcher really has to know his staff. Some guys you have to handle with kid gloves and some guys really need a kick in the pants."

A pitching coach will not go to the mound unless he has received permission from his manager or the manager has specifically asked him to talk to the pitcher. If the manager has sent him, he may very well be stalling for time until someone in the bull pen is ready to come in. Otherwise, says Mets' pitching coach Mel Stottlemyre, "It's because I've seen something in his delivery or want to remind him about something we've discussed. Or it may be to settle him down, make him aware of who the hitter is and what the right pitch to throw is."

Stottlemyre tries not to be humorous during such visits. "But I recognize [the pitcher] may be tired, so I may joke around and say, 'If you don't get this guy out, it's your last batter.'" The coach also tries not to be rough, "But sometimes we all need to be woken up."

If Stottlemyre and his pitcher don't talk on the mound, they may talk in the dugout between innings. It is usually the role of pitching coach rather than manager to discuss the game as it unfolds—what pitches were made in the last inning, what pitches might be made in the next inning. Some pitchers are so intense that they do not like to be disturbed by anyone, including teammates and pitching coaches. Says Tigers' pitching coach Billy Muffett, "I don't try to do much with them during the game. They've got enough on their minds." But other pitchers welcome communication. "Oh sure, the guys come up and talk," says Guidry. They ask, 'How you gonna pitch this guy? Where do you want me to play this guy?' You might joke around, break the monotony."

The fan who wishes to break the monotony might consider playing spy or detective and try to decode the signs being given by the human semaphore—the third-base coach. Actually, the coach is both receiver and transmitter, for he takes one set of signs sent to him by the manager in the dugout and then sends them along in a different code to batter and base runners. Such work is absolutely essential, for there is no way for a manager to come out of the dugout and tell his men at the plate and on the bases what he wants them to do. Explains Zimmer, "The third-base coach is responsible if a player doesn't get a sign. And if he doesn't get it, we're not playing the manager's game. The whole thing is to be able to relay to the players the way the manager wants to play the game."

Thus it was that when Pirates' manager Jim Leyland was the Chicago White Sox third-base coach, he would spend part of his off-season in front of a mirror, practicing his signs. Or that when the veteran coach Zimmer came to the Yankees from the Cubs in the middle of 1986, he worried for the first week whether he was faithfully conveying manager Lou

Piniella's messages. "It takes a while to feel accustomed out there," he admits.

There are any number of sign systems. At the simplest level, when a coach touches a particular place on his body or uniform, that may mean something to the batter and/or runners—hit and run, bunt, steal. If this is the simplest way to send a message, it is also the simplest way to have one intercepted (and the opposition is always trying to do that). More elaborate systems, therefore, have been developed. Zimmer explains the two major ones:

"There's the key, or indicator, system. This means if I'm sending signs for hit and run or bunt or steal, I can go through all kinds of signs—most of it is decoy anyway—but nothing is really on until I hit the key. The key could be anything, let's say touching my belt. So when I hit that key that alerts the hitter and runner that something is on if the next thing I touch is a sign. Let's say touching my shirt is the sign for hit and run. If I just hit my shirt nothing's on, but then if I hit three or four spots and then hit my belt [the key] that alerts them to watch for the next sign. So if I hit the shirt right after hitting the belt, that means the hit and run is on.

"There is also a system based on numbers. Say the hit and run is any time I hit two spots. So if I touched my hat and shirt—two spots—and stopped, that means hit and run. Let's say steal is three spots. If I go nose, hat, pants—three spots—and stop, that means steal."

While neither of these methods is terribly complex, Zimmer says that there are always two or three players in the starting lineup who have trouble with them. What does he do? "Try and make it as easy as possible. When a hitter goes to the plate, he's gotta be thinking, 'How do I hit this guy's 92-mile-an-hour fastball or his great curve?' I don't want him to be up there confused about my signs. So for the guys who have trouble, I'll use the same signs, but I won't use any of the decoys."

Because missing a sign can damage a team's effort (if a batter misses the sign to hit and run and doesn't swing at a pitch, the runner on first base might be an easy out at second base after he takes off expecting the man at the plate to swing), many teams will fine their hitters or runners if they are remiss. So everybody takes great care to learn signs, right? Well, not everybody. "They don't hit and run with me and I've been injured so often they don't want me to steal. So to tell you the truth, I don't even know our signs," says Brett.

Meanwhile, in the opposing dugout . . . the third-base coach is one of the most closely watched men on the field, for if a team can steal a sign it can indeed undermine the game a manager is trying to play. One of the best sign-stealers in recent years is Joe Nossek, who has coached for five different major-league clubs. He observes: "Stealing signs is important because if you can shut down the other team's running game, you're at a great advantage. I don't know whether the ability to steal signs is like a sixth sense or not. It took me a couple of years to get the hang of it. Success came when I was finally able to concentrate for an entire game. If you want to get the timing down between the manager, when he gives his signs to the coach, and the coach, when he gives it to the players, you have to maintain your concentration for nine innings. When I first started, I'd watch real well for three or four innings and then something would distract me. Then it seemed that whenever I was distracted, the sign had been given and I'd wasted all that time. You have to always be watching for it. Say your own manager is on the field arguing over a call; the other club may use that opportunity to slip in its signs.

"Sometimes you figure out the signs all of a sudden. You see the opposing coach do something different. You note that in your mind. Maybe nothing will happen the next two or three games, but then he'll give that same sign and everything will fall into place. You'll be able to steal a few signs then and get a couple of outs before they change. When I think I have a sign, I'll pass it along to the manager who'll signal it to our catcher. The manager might signal for the pitchout, for example. It's not something that's gonna win you a pennant, but every once in awhile you'll be able to get a big out. And if you can make the other team believe you have their signs, even if you don't, that can be valuable. The opposing manager might be afraid to put something on."

Of course, the opposing managers and third-base coaches whom Nossek refers to know that they are being put under the microscope, and they've developed their own system for detecting and foiling the sign-stealers. Some managers may use one set of signs for the first three batters in the lineup, another set for the next three batters, and a third set for the final trio.

More common is the use of the take-off sign. Says Zimmer, remembering his tenure as a third base coach, "If you hit a 'key' for the hit and run and the other team pitches out on you, your first thought is that they might have stolen the sign. Most of the time that's not the answer. It's just that they're smart enough to know that you play hit and run when so and so is at bat and they happened to guess right. But just to make sure, we have what we call a take-off sign. It could be anything, rubbing my hands across the letters, going to my nose. So if I think they have our sign for, say, the hit and run, I'll give the key, give the sign for hit and run, and then use the take-off sign [which calls the hit and run off]. Then, if they pitch out, I know they have our signs." At this point, Zimmer would change the signs, begin to sing in a different key.

There are certain situations in a game where the third-base coach will move to home plate and talk with his hitter rather than rely on signs. Why? "Say we have runners on first and second and the bunt is in order. Maybe our manager thinks the other team is going to use the wheel play [where the third baseman, who would ordinarily cover third base, charges, the shortstop covers third, the first baseman charges and the second baseman covers first]," says Zimmer. "Well, the manager will give me the bunt sign, but he'll also give me another sign that means to tell the batter we think the wheel is on. If the third baseman is charging there's no way you can execute the sacrifice bunt. But because the shortstop is moving over to third, that will leave a gap that our guy can slap the ball through. So I'll tell him that."

A third-base coach might also visit the batter if there are runners on first base and third base to clarify whether the manager wants a straight sacrifice bunt (to move the man from first to second while the runner on third stays put) or a squeeze (in which the runner on third heads for home). How does the runner on third receive his instructions? The coach will either take him aside, making sure the third baseman does not eavesdrop, or he might have a verbal cue. Explains Zimmer: "We may work it out so that if I use the runner's last name, it means the squeeze is on. So if I said, 'Be alive, so and so,' that means squeeze."

A coach can also use this verbal system to alert a batter that a particular pitch is coming. Sometimes catchers forget to hide their signs from the first-base or third-base coach and he can be almost certain whether a fastball or breaking ball is going to be thrown. But even if Zimmer thought he knew what kind of pitch was on the way, he wouldn't tell his batter. "I'd never want to be responsible for having signaled a curveball and then see a fastball come in high and tight on my hitter." If, however, a pitcher tipped a pitch by allowing Zimmer to see how he was gripping the ball, the coach might cue the man at the plate with a prearranged word. "Of course, the opposition catches on pretty fast to that kind of stuff," he says. Still, it can work. When he played for the San Francisco Giants, Willie Mays hit more than a few home runs because first-base coach Westrum was a great sign-stealer.

While the team at the plate is constantly communicating in sign language, so is the team on the field. As we have seen in chapter 4, the second baseman and shortstop—able to see the catcher's signs to the pitcher—will generally signal the first baseman and third baseman what pitch is on the way. How does the catcher's sign system work? In most cases, a catcher and pitcher work on the number system. If the catcher puts down one finger, he is calling for the fastball; two means curve; three means slider; and four fingers means change-up. As it is essential that the catcher know what pitch is coming, the pitcher will either "shake off" the sign—indicate no (usually by shaking his head, in which even the catcher will try again)—or nod his approval. (A fan can tell if a pitcher and catcher are in sync by watching to see how many times a pitcher shakes off his catcher. Sometimes you can even see frustration on the part of one or both men. But be aware, some wily pitchers, Tom Seaver was one, will sometimes merely pretend to shake off a sign to try to get one more edge on the batter.)

It figures that if a second baseman can see the catcher's fingers, so, too, can an opposing base runner standing on second base. To foil this would-be sign-stealer, catchers and pitchers generally employ either prearranged indicator signs or pump signs. Let's say "three" is the agreed upon indicator. If the catcher's signals one-four-three-two, he is calling for "two" (the curve), the number that followed the indicator "three."

In the pump system, a predetermined key number is used, let's say "two." The pitcher looks for the number of pumps the catcher makes with his fingers after he has given that key. If the catcher goes one-three-two-one-four-one and then stops, he is calling for number three, the slider, because he made three pumps after the key number. The number of fingers put down is just a decoy.

Being on the same wavelength here is terribly important. Here is an example from 1986: The Orioles are playing the Red Sox. It is the bottom of the first inning. The Red Sox lead, 1-0. There are two outs. The Sox's Bill Buckner is on second base, while the dangerous Don Baylor is at the plate. There are two strikes. Dempsey calls for a fastball and sets up on the inside of the plate, but Dixon throws a slider on the outside. Baylor swings and misses for strike three. But the slider catches Dempsey by surprise. It rolls all the way to the screen behind home plate and Baylor makes it to first base on the "dropped third strike." That would have been the third out, but instead of being in the dugout watching his team hit, Dixon is still on the mound. Sure enough, the next batter, Dwight Evans, hits a three-run homer, and the Sox go on to win 7-2.

The fan who looked into the Orioles' dugout when Dixon finally retired the side after Evans's blast might have observed an animated discussion between pitcher and catcher. "What's your sign?" one probably asked the other. And he wasn't referring to the Zodiac.

8

WHAT THE BOX SCORE DOESN'T REVEAL: WATCHING WITH THE EXPERTS

Where's a good place to sit and watch the game? Almost anywhere (another one of the joys of baseball), but some places are better than others. "I think you want to be elevated a bit, maybe halfway up the stands, not too close to the field," says Al Kaline, the Tigers Hall of Famer who now broadcasts games for Detroit. "It's great to be close where you're hearing all the action, but I think the best viewing area is up midway, so you're watching the ball at the proper level. Directly behind the plate is probably the best place, although you do have the screen to contend with."

Directly behind the plate, without any screen to contend with, in a comfortable, enclosed box with television set and telephone, is where the men who run baseball clubs usually sit, and it is where I'm sitting on a cool night in May. To write this chapter, I am watching a pro watch a game. My pro? Ken "Hawk" Harrelson, then White Sox Executive Vice President for Baseball Operations. (He would depart at the end of a disappointing season.) Harrelson is a wonderfully colorful character, given to flamboyant attire that usually includes cowboy hats and boots, but don't let his Western looks deceive. He knows the game—as player, broadcaster, and executive.

A little more about the man who will provide our commentary: as a player in the 1960s, Harrelson gained as much recognition for his off-the-field exploits as for his achievements between the white lines. While a member of the Kansas City Athletics, whose owner was the equally colorful Charles O. Finley, he delighted fans by taking pre-game sorties on the team's mascot mule (until the late Yankee great Roger Maris playfully threw a bat at the pair, causing Harrelson to swallow his tobacco and the mule to become a "bucking bronco"). On another occasion, under Finley's orders, he helped sneak a different mule onto the field during a game at Comiskey Park (Finley's response to a feud with the White Sox owner). Then in 1967, Harrelson openly criticized Finley's handling of the team. Finley was so infuriated that he put his ball player on irrevocable waivers, a status that in effect made Harrelson the game's first free agent. Free to make his own deal with whichever team he chose, he headed for Boston, arriving just in time to help the team to the pennant. Flourishing the next season in the hitter's paradise Fenway Park, he hit 35 home runs and led the major leagues in runs batted in.

The Hawk became a phenomenon in Boston, almost as big as the Refrigerator became in Chicago. There was a mod line of clothing, a television special, an autobiography (he appeared on the cover in the then-fashionable Nehru jacket), and a bachelor pad complete with circular bed and a houseboy, Wendell. Traded to Cleveland early in 1969 because the Red Sox were desperate for pitching, Harrelson was so devastated that he refused to report until persuaded by a personal audience with then Baseball Commissioner Bowie Kuhn . . . and additional cash. (Red Sox fans were so angry that they picketed Fenway Park, and Wendell was so distraught that he suffered a mild heart attack.) He hit 30 home runs that season, but a leg injury the next season eventually cut short his career.

These trials and tribulations notwithstanding, Harrelson was always a devoted student of baseball, staying long hours after games to discuss strategy with coaches and teammates. (He laments that the days of postgame skull sessions are past and that most players today hustle out of the clubhouse as soon as they've showered.) "I always knew I'd either be a manager, general manager, or owner after I stopped playing," he remembers. It took 13 years and didn't last too long.

After retiring from baseball, he attempted to play on the professional golf tour, but failed after three years. "I had the physical abilities, but not the mental discipline," he says. He was much more successful in his next jobs, broadcasting baseball games for the Red Sox and then the White Sox. After turning down a handful of offers to manage and failing in an attempt to buy a major-league franchise, Harrelson left television to run the baseball side of the White Sox at the end of the 1985 season. The going was rough in 1986. Initially, Harrelson and then Sox manager Tony LaRussa clashed over any number of issues, including Harrelson's novel hiring of Moe Drabowsky to be a relief-pitching coach and his firing of many minor-league coaches. The conflict reached a head in early May with the Sox foundering both on the field (with a 7 win 18 loss record) and off. A press conference was called and almost everyone expected Harrelson to fire LaRussa and replace him with Billy Martin. Instead the Hawk cried "Mea culpa!" and gave LaRussa a vote of confidence. Although LaRussa was eventually replaced by Jim Fregosi, on this night on which we watch the game, he is still the manager. The White Sox have won six games in a row to make their record 16-20. They face the 1985 A.L. East champion Toronto Blue Jays who have struggled to a 17-22 start.

The starting pitchers tonight make for an interesting matchup. Doyle Alexander (subsequently traded to Atlanta and then picked up by Detroit) will take the mound for the

Blue Jays. Alexander has had arm trouble in the past that threatened his career and he relies on guile rather than speed. He has won 155 games. A well traveled ball player, he is as of tonight one of only two active major leaguers to have registered a win against every major-league club. (Don Sutton is the other.) In 1985, he won 17 games, and his 1986 record to date is 3-1.

Pitching for the White Sox will be Neil Allen, 1-0 this season and 47-56 in a six-year career. Allen, who was a premier reliever in the National League before falling on hard times, was acquired from the Yankees during the off-season and is a Harrelson gamble. He has not shown much since the Mets traded him to the Cardinals for Keith Hernandez in 1983. He began the season in the Sox bull pen, but was moved to the starting rotation three weeks ago. He has been impressive in each of his three starts, giving up just 15 hits and three earned runs in 21 innings. (And he would be even more impressive as the season progressed—at one time recording consecutive shutouts.) While possessed of a fine fastball, Allen relies equally heavily on the breaking ball. But he is laboring under a burden this evening. According to a newspaper column in this morning's paper, his wife has filed for divorce and retained famed California attorney Marvin Mitchelson.

Toronto Blue Jays Vs. Chicago White Sox: May 21, 1986

First inning. The Blue Jays send Damaso Garcia, Lloyd Moseby, and Rance Mulliniks to the plate. Harrelson is concentrating on one thing: "Allen's curveball. He has to get that over to be effective." Of particular concern is whether the umpire behind the plate will "give him" the curve—call it a strike—for strike zones vary somewhat from umpire to umpire, particularly with a pitch that curves in so dramatically at the last second. "There are four or five umps who might not give it to him," says Harrelson. "But Steve Palermo [tonight's umpire] is a good one." Although Harrelson winces on a couple of curves that Palermo calls balls, Allen survives the calls and makes it through the first inning un- scathed, retiring all three men and striking out one.

As the Blue Jays take their positions, Harrelson marvels at the outfield—George Bell in left, Moseby in center, and Jesse Barfield in right. Each is an excellent defensive player and can hit for power and average. (Indeed, Moseby and Barfield were named to the American League All-Star team later in the season.) The Sox leadoff man is John Cangelosi, another Harrelson gamble. Cangelosi, the closest thing in the game to a sprite, came to spring training given little chance of making the team, but performed so well that the Hawk released last year's starter Rudy Law and sent his heir apparent, Daryl Boston, to the minors.

Although he is the smallest man in the league, Cangelosi compensates with determination and speed. He is second in the league in stolen bases, having already swiped 19 this early in the season. He starts things off for the Sox by sing- ling. Cangelosi is followed in the lineup tonight by Ozzie Guillen, the flamboyant shortstop, who was Rookie of the Year in 1985. Guillen usually bats eighth or ninth in the order. "I like him batting second, but I'll admit that he hasn't shown that much discipline to bat there yet," says Harrelson.

What does he mean? As the leadoff hitter is usually a man with basestealing potential, the man who bats second must have the patience to take pitches even if they are strikes when the leadoff man gets on base so he can try to steal. Guillen is, however, a free swinger who frequently chases the first pitch whether it is a strike or not. Perhaps such a lineup move will make him more discriminating in time. But he is not selective now, swinging at the first offering and flying out to center.

This brings the Sox All-Star right fielder Harold Baines to the plate. Baines does take a pitch, and Cangelosi promptly steals second. Cangelosi, who has already stolen third base several times this season, now takes a bold lead off second. Alexander whirls and fires to the shortstop, who has ducked in behind Cangelosi. Cangelosi dives back head first and is safe. Says Harrelson, "On a play like that the man covering second [in this case, the shortstop] should put his knee down and block the base. But the only guy who does that is Bobby Grich [the California Angels' second baseman, now retired]." It makes sense. A catcher will block home plate when a runner approaches, but when the shortstop or second baseman covers, he almost always stands off to the side. Then again, the catcher has shin guards. What if Cangelosi comes back to the base spikes first instead of head first? "You roll the dice," says Harrelson, who during his early years in baseball spent off-seasons playing pool and finding golf games to supplement his income.

Baines now singles to shallow left field. Most runners would stop at third, but Cangelosi doesn't even think about slowing down as he heads for home. He scores, but some in Harrelson's box doubt whether he should have tried. "When you have that kind of speed you make the left fielder throw you out," Harrelson says, then adds, "You can't beat speed." The Blue Jays, figuring they had a play on Cangelosi, did not cut off the throw, so Baines is able to take second base on the throw to the plate.

Greg Walker flies out to right, bringing up Carlton Fisk. "I'd like to see him hit a little duck snort to right," says Harrelson. Toronto's scouting reports must indicate that the right-handed Fisk is strictly a pull hitter and will hit it to left field; the Jays are giving Fisk a great deal of room in right. But now Harrelson notices something (something the diligent fan can look for) that tips off Fisk's strategy. "Look how he's standing. He's too close to the plate to go to right," says Harrelson. He's correct. Fisk grounds out to third base to end the inning.

Second inning.   Allen is not getting the strike call on his curveball. Can that bother a pitcher? "Sure, anyone can get rattled," says Harrelson. After walking the first man up, Willie Upshaw, Allen leaves the mound and heads for the Sox dugout. Rarely will a player do this. "I hope it's just an upset stomach," says Harrelson. The Sox have already been forced to put two of their top pitchers, Tom Seaver and Floyd Bannister, on the disabled list. Allen returns somewhat rejuvenated, and despite a wild pitch that sends Upshaw to second, he strikes out the dangerous Bell with a curve. Harrelson marvels: "When he's on he can get the curveball up and still get it over." He then remembers a story about another player who had to leave the field in the middle of an inning. It happened in the early Sixties when the Athletics journeyed to Yankee Stadium. It was the first time in the hallowed park for one of Harrelson's teammates and to cap it off, the Yanks' legendary Whitey Ford was pitching. The ball player, known more for his glove than his bat, was in awe, but managed to hit a double off Ford. No sooner had he bounced up from his slide into second base than he called time and ran into the dugout. Was he hurt? "No," says Harrelson, laughing, "he was so excited he'd crapped in his pants."

The talented Barfield is at the plate. Allen is again having trouble with his curve and issues his second walk of the inning. Harrelson shakes his head. (Remember, all pitchers say that in order to be effective, you can't give up too many walks.) The next batter up is Cliff Johnson, the veteran designated hitter, who still has great power. After the first pitch, umpire Palermo stops play, indicates that Johnson has not kept his feet in the batter's box as the rules require, and directs him to do so. Johnson looks at him in disbelief and a heated argument ensues. This marks the second time play has been interrupted, and Harrelson begins to look for a full moon.

The Hawk has sympathy for Johnson. "I used to stay way back in the box, too," he says. "I'd get in arguments all the time, but with the good umps you don't even try to argue or get away with it." But there is no sympathy for what happens next. Johnson steps back in and promptly hits a home run. "Fastball right over the middle of the plate," moans Harrelson. "That's what you end up throwing when you can't get your curveball over for strikes."

Allen runs the count to 3-0 on the next batter, Ernie Whitt, and then, again forced to throw a strike because he is behind in the count, gives up a triple. He retires Tony Fernandez, but Garcia hits a double to score Whitt. The Blue Jays lead 4-1. At this point, LaRussa replaces Allen with Dave Schmidt, another off-season acquisition. Harrelson picks up the phone in his box. Earlier tonight he had used it to find out how the minor-league teams were doing and later he will take a call from owner Eddie Einhorn, who is out of town. Now, however, he wants to talk to the dugout to find out if there is anything physical bothering Allen. There is. The pitcher hurt his groin running to cover first base on a play in the first inning. Harrelson sighs. All he needs is a third starter to join Seaver and Bannister on the sidelines. We frequently hear about players "playing hurt," staying in the game despite injury. Harrelson is asked if a pitcher with a pulled groin should play hurt. "No," he says emphatically. "You can't fight through that kind of injury. You should only stay in if it's something that can't get any worse."

The fans in the park will have to wait until they read their morning newspapers to realize that Allen's ineffective performance may be attributable in large part to physical injury. (I don't know why ball clubs don't use their fancy scoreboards to immediately convey more information, such as injury reports, to those in the park.) On other occasions, those of us in our seats will never know that a particular player is playing hurt (remember Mets' trainer Steve Garland's observations in Chapter 1). Most players are so competitive that they would rather stay in the lineup than sit on the bench and are more than willing to hear a few boos if they don't perform up to the fans' expectations. (In general, the praise of their peers is much more important to players than the praise of the press or of fans.) As those of us in the seats might not know that a player has a bad back or an upset stomach, or is going through a messy divorce, Tigers' manager Sparky Anderson asks for our patience: "The fans have to understand that a lot of things can be going on with players. Someone might have financial problems or family problems." How does Anderson know? "I don't ever walk through the clubhouse that my eyes don't watch. I've been in this so long, I know what to look for. It's a feeling. I know when there's a little group together, when something is going on. I'll slowly browse by and catch a little word. All I have to do is hear one or two words and I can put the whole story together."

In the game, Schmidt (now with Baltimore) retires Moseby for the third out.

As the Sox come up, Harrelson worries about giving the wily Alexander a big lead early in the game. "He can really screw around with you, really play tricks changing speeds, showing you different deliveries. When you pitch like he does with that herky-jerky motion, the plate becomes a little wider [because hitters are so off balance]." Does the Hawk think Alexander fits the classic definition of a pitcher who throws "junk"? Harrelson: "Yes, with that motion. The reason he's a pretty good pitcher is because he's so deceptive." Harrelson remembers Stu Miller, who lasted 16 years on major-league pitching mounds. "He didn't throw anything except junk, but because of the motion of his head [he demonstrates, bobbing his noggin up and down, this way and that way], he was really successful." He laughs, "If you do that too quick you get a headache."

Rookie Bobby Bonilla (later traded to Pittsburgh) leads off with a single for the Sox. Ron Kittle comes to the plate. Kittle (now with the Cleveland Indians) is a likable character who drives fans crazy because he is usually either on a home run streak or striking out with annoying regularity. He has hit 93 home runs in his first three years, but has also struck out 375 times. Unfortunately, it has been strikeout time lately—Kittle has not hit a home run in three weeks and has already fanned 34 times in only 113 at bats.

In Chicago, one of the first questions fans used to ask on many sports call-in shows is, "What's wrong with Kittle?" The fan who has been watching Kittle closely the past few games should have been able to see what Harrelson now describes: "You don't need a timer to tell that his bat speed is appreciably slower." This means the right-handed hitter is late getting his bat around, so he either misses the pitch completely or by the time he does make contact he is unable to pull the ball to left field either for base hits or home runs. Many of his outs have been weak taps or popups to the right side of the infield. Someone in Harrelson's box suggests that Kittle should forget about pulling the ball and intentionally try to go to right field with the pitch. Harrelson disagrees, noting that this would require consciously trying to slow down his swing. "That would make his bat even slower, and besides when you're struggling you don't even think about making changes like that." Kittle remains true to recent form and pops up to the second baseman, but Wayne Tolleson (since traded to the Yankees) and Cangelosi each single with two outs to put another run across before the inning ends. The Blue Jays lead 4-2.

Third inning. Harrelson on Schmidt, who entered the game with a poor 7.00 earned run average and has been struggling most of the year: "In spring training, his fastball moved, but lately it hasn't been doing anything." Since movement is as important as velocity, if a fastball doesn't move—go up or down, in or out—the batters will have a much easier time of it. Schmidt's delivery is different than that of most pitchers. Allen, for example, has a high leg kick as he delivers the ball, but Schmidt stands almost straight up. Says Harrelson, "The guys who throw straight up usually rush a bit." (Rushing too much can cause the pitch to stay up high—where most batters like it.) Schmidt gives up a one-out triple to Upshaw, but pitches his way out of trouble by retiring the next two men. A pleased Harrelson admits that if a team is to compete for a championship, it must have a strong bull pen.

The Sox go down in order, the only notable occurrence a long drive by Fisk caught by Bell against the left-field wall. During the off-season, the Sox moved home plate back about eight feet, making it a bit more difficult for hitters to get the ball out of the park. Fisk's out would have been a home run in 1985. One of baseball's charms is that, unlike football with its standard field, and basketball with its standard court, the dimensions vary from park to park and each park has its own eccentricities—stands that jut out almost to the foul lines, corners that make for odd bounces. On occasion, teams tinker with such geometry—moving the plate closer to the fences or farther away, raising or lowering outfield walls—in an effort to take advantage of what they perceive to be their strengths or diminish what they perceive to be their weaknesses. Going into 1986, one of the Sox's strengths was that they had four solid home run threats in Baines, Walker, Fisk, and Kittle. But one of the team's weaknesses was that its pitching staff gave up too many homers. Harrelson determined that only a few of the home runs his sluggers hit were "cheap" and that adding a few feet wouldn't affect them as much as it would opposing players, whom he felt hit a lot more cheap round-trippers. The results six weeks into the season: "I think we've lost about eight home runs and our opponents have lost about 14," says Harrelson. "It's really helped our [pitcher] Rich Dotson. There've been five balls hit against him which probably would have been out of the park last year."

Fourth inning.   Schmidt retires the Blue Jays in order. With one out in the Sox half of the inning, Kittle singles to right center field. Had his bat been quicker, Harrelson says, he could have pulled it. He was just slow getting to the pitch. Still, Harrelson marvels at Kittle's strength. "Most guys would have just hit a little flare on that pitch, but he's so strong, he hit it well."

Fifth inning.   The score remains 4-2. Schmidt strikes out leadoff batter Garcia with a palm ball, a variation of the change-up. Harrelson is delighted to see this. "That's what we got him for," he says. "But he hasn't been throwing it." Why? There is only so much a general manager can do with respect to on-the-field strategy. "I've asked the same question," he says.

The next batter, Moseby, singles. Moseby is possessed of

both power and speed, and Harrelson immediately predicts, "He's gonna try and steal second, it's only a matter of when." Someone in the box complains that the Sox pitchers can't seem to pick anyone off first base. Harrelson: "Not too many teams have anyone that can. It's amazing. In the past that was one of the things teams worked on most. It's not worked on much anymore, but we've started teaching it again in the minors."

While this answer might make Harrelson sound like one of those former ball players who bemoans the good old days when baseball was better, he isn't. He thinks players today are more talented than they were in the past, but notes that they are reaching the major leagues at an earlier age than a generation or even a decade ago. As a result, they receive less minor-league instruction in the fundamentals of the game and frequently reach the big leagues deficient in such basics as the pickoff. Harrelson has a suggestion for those who don't have good moves. "Just hold the ball, hold it, hold it [to throw off the timing of the runner on first]." This brings to mind another Whitey Ford story. When the Yankees faced the Dodgers in the 1963 World Series, all eyes were on the National League-leading stealer Maury Wills, who the year before had become the first man ever to steal 100 bases in a season. The Yankees' pitchers were understandably worried about Wills, who in addition to being very fast was expert at reading pitchers' moves. Ford's solution: He never showed him the move, never once threw over to first base, and thus prevented him from measuring how big a lead to take. Wills never stole a base against him in the Series.

Tonight, Harrelson is right about Moseby. The runner gets a huge jump on the next pitch and takes off. Fortunately for the Sox, Mulliniks fouls the ball off. Moseby, who had slid into second, returns to first base on the foul. Harrelson observes that with such a big jump, "Moseby could have gone in to second standing if he'd have picked the ball up." (Remember Joe Morgan on picking the ball up in chapter 4. If a runner can go in standing, he is in a much better position to advance an extra base on an errant throw or a base hit. "We're teaching that in the minors, too," says Harrelson.

Moseby seems to be distracting Schmidt. He doesn't attempt another steal, but Mulliniks singles. Says Harrelson, "There's still a basic rule. You gotta get the hitter." Schmidt settles down and retires the side.

Cangelosi leads off with his third straight single. This time he tries to steal on the first pitch. The Blue Jays, sensing that he might do so, have pitched out, but the catcher's throw travels wildly into the outfield, allowing Cangelosi to take third. Guillen does his job by keeping the ball on the right side of the field; his grounder to the second baseman allows Cangelosi to score. Baines follows with a single. Walker gets a fastball where any hitter would want it—right over the plate—but fouls it straight back. As Ted Williams notes, this is sometimes a sign that the batter just missed a good hit. "He is getting some good pitches to hit," says Harrelson. The next pitch falls into that category, and Walker doubles. Baines stops at third. Fisk fails to drive in the runners, then Bonilla hits a shot down the third-base line that is barely foul. Harrelson is as exasperated as any fan. A few inches the other way and the Sox would be leading 5-4 instead of trailing 4-3.

Sixth inning. The game is already over two hours old. "It's been out of sync from the beginning," says Harrelson. "There's no flow." Football commentators frequently talk about "momentum." But football is a more emotional game. "Flow" seems more appropriate for baseball. Can you get a feel for the way the action will unfold, for the final result based on what happens earlier? "Sometimes," says Harrelson.

Kaline expands here: "You can develop a picture. If you keep letting the starting pitcher off the hook, and you always have a couple of men on base, that's really not good because eventually that pitcher is going to be taken out for another one and you're gonna have squandered all those opportunities to get to the starting pitcher. And most teams now have excellent help in the bull pen from the seventh inning on. So if a team doesn't score runs early, odds are they aren't gonna score many runs or have too many big innings from the 7th inning on when a new pitcher comes in."

Sparky Anderson's explanation is almost mystical. "I watched a game yesterday," he said early last season. "The Cubs were playing Montreal. I knew the Cubs were a loser. In the 11th inning, they have runners on first and second with nobody out, and they don't move a soul. They end up the inning with men on first and second. I said, 'They're gonna lose. It's just a matter of innings. It might go 13, 14, 15, but they're gonna lose. You can't miss those shots in extra innings and still win. The party's over.' And sure enough, they lost in the bottom of the 11th.

"Sometimes you have a feeling when you're ahead after seven innings. You know you're gonna lose. You can see what's happening. It's just a matter of time. You're playing a ball club that's hot and has been coming from behind. And they know they can win. And there are also times I know my club is not gonna lose. They may be down 5-1 in the 3rd inning, but I can feel things are going well for us."

Stranded runners, as both Kaline and Anderson note, are the bane of a ball club, but Harrelson makes sense when he says, "I'd rather see us stranding runners than not have any runners on."

Although tonight's game is out of sync and seems to be taking forever, Harrelson wishes it were going even more slowly. "If you're ahead in a game, you want to speed it up. If you're behind you want to slow it down. The team with the lead hates to be slowed down; it gets them off kilter." Thus it was that Dick Howser was disturbed by the delays in Game 7 of the 1985 World Series (arguments with the umpires by St. Louis pitcher Andujar and manager Herzog). His team had a big lead; he didn't want the action to stop.

Harrelson gets his wish. The game slows down even more. But the circumstances are not to his liking. Schmidt, who has been pitching so well tonight, has to leave the game because his back is giving him trouble. The thought of losing two pitchers to injury in one night when the team already has lost two is too much for Harrelson, who leaves the box and spends the rest of the game pacing about the park.

Seventh through ninth innings. Harrelson returns briefly in the 7th inning, the score now tied at 4-4. Jim Acker, a hard-throwing right-hander, has replaced Alexander. Bonilla comes to the plate with two men on base and one out. Harrelson, fearing Bonilla's inability to handle Acker's fastball, says he'd like to see Jerry Hairston pinch-hit for the rookie. But LaRussa leaves Bonilla in. He pops out, as does Kittle, and the Sox don't score.

In the 8th inning, the Sox have another opportunity. They have a runner on third base with one out. Cangelosi, a switch hitter, is due up. He has three hits in four at bats. The Blue Jays bring in relief ace Mark Eichhorn. Is now the right time to send in Hairston, the league's preeminent pinch hitter? LaRussa thinks so. Hairston responds with a single, and the Sox go on to win 5-4.

It's my hope that recapitulations like the above and those described in the previous seven chapters have increased your understanding and appreciation of the game of baseball and may even change the way you watch a game. I'd be the last to suggest that you should constantly take your eye off the ball; but I'd be the first to agree that if you periodically widen your scope, you'll see a lot more. Says Haywood Sullivan, the former big-league catcher and managing partner of the Red Sox: "Baseball is just like football or basketball where if the average fan could watch some of the line play or backcourt play, he'd get a little more education than just one thing going on. For instance, when the ball is hit to an infielder, take your eyes off the infielder and watch what the outfielders are doing. See if they're backing up the bases."

It seems to me that many people come to the park and watch a game as if they were watching on television, focusing almost entirely on the pitcher and hitter and batted ball. Yes, this is where the plot usually unfolds. But don't limit yourself. Enjoy the subplots that add to the drama: out- fielders backing up infielders; infielders moving in anticipa- tion of particular pitches; catchers controlling the tempo of the game; hitters trying to get their timing down in the on- deck circle; base runners trying to decipher pitchers' moves; coaches giving and stealing signs; men on the bench trying to stay loose and help in any way possible; umpires talking with catcher, hitter, and pitcher; and the manager, flamboyant or laid back, setting the tone and strategy for his ball club. There are more than three rings to this circus.

When you do concentrate on the "center ring" be aware of the cat-and-mouse game the man on the mound and the man at the plate are playing. Watch the sequence and location of the pitcher's pitches, and watch how the batter responds. Keep your eye on the pitcher after he delivers the ball and see how he follows through; observe the batter's hands and head and hips after he makes contact. Compare the different deliveries of pitchers and the different stances of hitters. Do flamethrowers look different from finesse pitchers? Do singles hitters look different than home run threats? Watch, too, the rapport between pitcher and catcher.

Your preparation for all of this can begin before the game (just as a team's preparation begins long before taking the field). You don't have to get into the habit, à la the Mets' Bud Harrelson, of burying your head in the box scores at the breakfast table. But you might find the game more enjoyable if you scan this immensely revealing resource, read the accounts of games involving your hometown heroes, look in the daily newspaper to find statistics revealing how your team and its individuals are faring, and bone up on the opposition by looking at its box scores and reading the brief stories about its recent games that virtually every newspaper now runs.

If you can, come to the park early and watch batting practice, à la wise pitching coaches like Mel Stottlemyre and savvy outfielders like Dave Winfield. See what each batter is trying to do when he takes his swings, make a mental note of it, and see what he tries to do during the game. Watch the fielders reconnoiter the park—its singular bounces and caroms and its changing wind and sun or lights—then see if their field work pays off once the game starts.

If you don't normally score the game, try doing so to see if it keeps you more involved in the proceedings, reveals hitherto unseen patterns about, for example, the number of men a particular pitcher retires on ground balls as opposed to fly balls. If you normally score the game, experiment by doing so in more detail. How? Start by recording whether the first pitch to each batter is a ball or strike. Then, chart the success of the pitcher (and hitter) based on that first pitch. Statistics indicate that the pitcher is significantly more successful if he gets his first pitch over for a strike. Recent studies show that over 80 percent of walks occur when the first pitch is a ball, and that a hitter batting eighth in the lineup (a spot reserved for a weaker batter) with a 1-0 count is more likely to get a hit than a hitter batting fourth (a spot reserved for a better batter) who is behind 0-1.

You might also record the count on which each at bat is decided. For example, make a note that the batter was retired on, say, a 1-2 pitch, or, say, that he got a double on a 2-1 pitch. Then at the end of the day, compare the pitcher's effectiveness vis à vis men he got behind on the count to and men he got ahead of.

If you get hooked on scoring the game, you might consider saving your scorecards to observe even larger patterns. For example: who are the hitters that really come through in the clutch? Says Kaline, "Base hits are nice and everyone likes to get them, but it's really important *when* a guy gets a base hit, *when* a guy hits a home run. Does it come at a time when it really means something or is it late in the game when the team is already way behind or way ahead? If the team is one run behind and the man leading off the inning is somehow able to get on base, that's important."

Whether you score the game or not, be aware of the scoreboard. Baseball people have an expression, "Play the scoreboard." In other words, at all times know the score, the number of outs, the number of balls and strikes, where any base runners might be. Says Duke Sims, a former big-league catcher and minor-league manager: "Most of the time the scoreboard dictates what you can do, whether you're behind one or two runs, or up one or two. The concept of the game is you want to get as many runs as early as you can, because for every one you pick up in front, you don't have to pick it up in back. So a lot of the back end of the game becomes a conservative, safety-first position, both offensively and defensively, because you can't afford to run yourself out of an inning and you don't want to make a mistake that would take a big inning away where you can ice a game. So a lot of the time you'll see things going on in the first six innings that you won't see in the last third."

A lot of the time, but not *all* the time. Sims continues: "There are certain things good managers do early in a game that they almost never do in the late part, but when you do see them do it in the late part it surprises everybody and they may steal a run and win a ball game. Example: You may hit and run on the first pitch 20 times in a row, and then maybe the count will be 2 and 0 with a power hitter up (an unlikely hit-and-run situation) and you'll hit and run with him or at least have your guys moving so that if he gets an extra-base hit they can score."

Of course as interesting as the scorecard and scoreboard may be, it is the players who star in the drama that remain the center of attention. Observe the different styles and personalities of the men on the field (the deliberate pace of baseball affords the luxury of doing this). Here is Reggie Jackson in 1986, shortly before his Angels take the field against the White Sox on what he will watch from the dugout: "I love to watch the players on the other team. So tonight, I'll watch Harold Baines, a great hitter. I'll watch his fundamentals, his smooth swing, his stance, how he approaches the baseball. I'll even watch how Baines is not very emotional, how he maintains his composure. I'll watch Ozzie Guillen at shortstop, how he fields the ball, his movements on the field. I'll watch the flamboyant, hot-dog style of Julio Cruz at second base. I don't hit Tom Seaver well, but I enjoy watching him pitch because he's a Hall of Famer and you don't get that opportunity very much. With Seaver, for example, you can see early how well he's pitching. You can see if he looks tired, if he's on top of his game. I don't really like his personality on the mound, but I admire his pitching style, his control of his abilities."

There are bound to be slow spots in any sporting event, but if you keep your eyes open at a baseball game there is always something interesting to see. When Jackson is bored, he watches players' mannerisms: "Watch Dick Schofield play shortstop for us. He has a regimen that he goes through [demonstrating]: he touches the front of his cap, he pounds his glove, he goes to his cup, he goes to his knee, he hits his glove, he goes back to his knee—now he's ready. Every game. Every day. And there are a lot of players who do that. All of your great players have a certain thing that they do, that when they don't do it, they're uncomfortable."

Will the fan who watches Jackson closely see a similar regimen? "Yes," says the slugger. "I have something when I'm hitting, but it's so much a part of me I don't really know it. I touch my glasses, I mash my helmet with my hand, I spit a few times through my teeth. I'm not really aware of it, but if someone would stop me from doing it, I'd probably be uncomfortable."

A month after the Toronto-Chicago game chronicled above, I found myself on assignment in the visiting Seattle Mariners' clubhouse at Comiskey Park and by chance had the opportunity to watch an inning of a ball game with the team.

It is a steamy June afternoon, and the Mariners have just returned to the locker room from batting practice. They have about an hour and 15 minutes to kill before taking the field against the White Sox. Ken Phelps, the Mariners' extroverted designated hitter (now with the Yankees), climbs up on a chair and turns on the television. The consensus in the locker room is to watch "American Bandstand," and several players sit in front of their lockers admiring Belinda Carlisle, the former lead singer of the Go Gos (the rock group, not the Go-Go White Sox of 1959) sing her latest single. Conversation centers on Ms. Carlisle's trimmed-down figure and the fact that she dated Mike Marshall of the Los Angeles Dodgers. Phelps hams it up. Pointing to various women on the screen, he tells them where he'll meet them after today's ball game.

The show ends before Phelps can elicit any responses from the young women on the screen, and he obliges his teammates by switching to NBC for the Game of the Week. The Orioles are playing the Red Sox. Roger Clemens, the best pitcher in baseball in 1986 (his record at this juncture is 12-0) is pitching for Boston. One of his more impressive victories came earlier in the season when he struck out a record 20 Mariners in nine innings. Learning Clemens is on the mound, every Mariner pulls up a chair. The players talk in superlatives about their historic meeting with Clemens. Rookie Danny Tartabull tells another rookie, Harold Reynolds, who has recently joined the team, "It was unbelievable. He was throwing gas, man. His slider was 90 miles an hour [most pitchers can't even throw the fastball this fast]. Pure heat."

Clemens retires the Orioles in the first inning, striking out the first two men he faces. There is some discussion among the Seattle players about whether his fastball (gauged at a remarkable 95 mph by NBC) is going straight over the middle of the plate or "catching the black"—the outer border of the plate. Most of the hitters think it's on the black, but pitcher Jim Beattie, who seems to have the last word, insists it is down the middle. "Television just distorts it," he explains. (He's right. Because the camera is not directly over the pitcher's shoulder this is inevitable.)

Ken Dixon is pitching for Baltimore. He is a competent

pitcher this season, but he has already given up an astounding 22 home runs in only 82 innings. "Who hasn't hit a dinger [home run] for a while?" asks one Mariner. "It might be his lucky day."

Marty Barrett leads off for Boston. Earlier in the year, he was batting lower in the order and was hitting quite well. He has tailed off of late. "That's because he's moved up to leadoff," explains a now-serious Phelps. "When you're low in the order, you may go 1 for 3, but when you're leading off, you get more at bats and those can turn into 1 for 4 and 1 for 5 days." Barrett strikes out. The next batter, Ed Romero, hits a grounder off Dixon's glove. Second baseman Juan Bonilla chases the deflected ball (which Dixon, perhaps, should have fielded cleanly) and appears to throw Romero out, but the umpire rules him safe.

The Mariners hoot like Orioles' fans when the replay shows Romero was out. They suggest that the umpire made up his mind based on past experience rather than the present facts. "The ump didn't think Bonilla could get to it," says Dave Henderson. Says Reynolds, "No, he didn't think [first baseman] Eddie Murray could get in position to take Bonilla's throw." Says Steve Fireovid, "I respect the umps, but those replays will kill 'em."

Instead of two out and nobody on base, there is one out and a runner on first. Bill Buckner comes to the plate. One of baseball's most consistent hitters, his average is an uncharacteristically low .237. "What you doing hitting .237, Billy Buck?" Henderson, who would later be traded to the Red Sox, asks the screen (eliciting the same response Phelps got earlier). Buckner, as previously mentioned, is a recent convert to the Lau-Hriniak school of hitting. He shows his stuff by hitting what looks to be an excellent low and away two-strike pitch for a double. "How'd he get that?" marvels Henderson.

"You can't pitch that way to him," says a teammate.

The powerful Jim Rice is up. Rice's stance places him almost right over the plate. "Look how close he is to home," says one Mariner. "You gotta come inside on him," says another. Most pitchers feel that home plate belongs to them as much as it does the batter, and if a man crowds it as much as Rice now does, they'll back him off with an inside fastball. But Dixon's first pitch is outside. "C'mon, man, come inside. You gotta break his lumber." Dixon stays outside, but manages to retire Rice.

This brings up Don Baylor who reaches first on a dropped third strike. The pitch, as described in Chapter 7, appears to fool catcher Rick Dempsey. But before this happens, the Mariners exhort Dixon to come inside on the hitter, who crowds home plate even more than Rice. "Look at that front foot. It's almost on the plate. You gotta throw in, man," someone yells.

Initially, there is some debate among the players about whether the mix-up is the fault of Dixon or Dempsey. Dixon has his defenders, who point to circumstantial evidence. "If it had been Dixon's fault, Dempsey would have gone out to the mound right away to chew him out," says a player. But most of the Mariners side with the veteran catcher, citing a replay showing him setting up one place and the ball going elsewhere. (My theory, never substantiated: with a runner on second, Dempsey changed the signs so that the runner wouldn't steal them, then Dixon nodded his approval based on the discarded system.)

When the next batter, Lau-Hriniak devotee Evans, comes to the plate, a few Mariners mock him. "He's so mechanical," says a player. "Everything has to be just right. I gotta have my foot just right, my bat just right, the black lines under my eyes [painted on to lessen the sun's glare] just right."

Maybe someone on the screen finally heard the Mariners. Evans promptly hits a three-run homer. Says Beattie: "Dixon threw it low and in when the catcher had set up away."

Says a teammate: "Another dinger off Dixon."

Tomorrow, players around the American League will pick up their newspapers, turn to the box score and see that both Clemens and Dixon pitched according to their form. They will construct mental pictures of the game so that they will be better prepared when next they face the Orioles or the Red Sox. But the box score won't reveal what they would have seen had they watched the game closely. Namely, that the Red Sox won the game because they were given five outs in the first inning. If Dixon had fielded Romero's ground ball cleanly (or if the umpire had made the right call at first base), if pitcher and catcher had not botched Baylor's third strike, Evans would never have come to the plate in the inning. Give a team three outs and it might not score; give it five and the odds are it will. That's just common sense. And perhaps one of the reasons baseball is so appealing is because it does make sense. The more we know about what is happening both on the field and behind the scenes, the more sense the game makes.

We began with an epigram from author and Red Sox watcher, George V. Higgins: "Baseball, like sex and religion, is a complicated game to play, but not hard to understand." Yes. Especially, if you know what to watch for.

9
WATCHING THE PLAYERS: THE ULTIMATE LESSON

Ask Reggie Jackson what he watched from the bench during a game, and he had a simple, one word answer, "Players." He is not alone. For most of us, watching baseball is watching individuals excel as individuals while playing a team sport.

In some ways the view I have presented of the game up to this point is reminiscent of a cubist painting. Here on the canvas we have a batter's head, there a base-runner's feet, there a fielder's glove, and over there a pitcher's belt buckle and twitching rear end! While it may be these fragments, these subtleties of hitting, running, fielding, and pitching that make baseball so intellectually appealing to us, it remains the players who grab our attention, excite us in the gut, cause us to stay in the ball park like kids long after the action is over just to express our appreciation and love.

What is it like to be a ball player? How does a player make it to the major leagues? What goes on before, during, and after a ball game? No book about watching baseball would be complete without a chapter that answers these questions, a chapter on watching and getting to know players. We need a traditional portrait to complement our abstract painting.

Almost all of us grew up playing baseball, and yet at any one time only an elite 624 are major leaguers. Within this elite there is, in effect, a super elite. Players with what is best described as "presence." Players so magnetic that we cannot take our eyes off them—whether it be because of their muscle or their grace, their flamboyance or their cool, their obvious hustle or their seeming effortlessness.

We all have our favorites. The player who has held a spell over me for the last several seasons is Carlton Fisk. At 6'2", 230 pounds, he would be hard to ignore in any arena. And with the numbers he has posted over his career (only two catchers in the history of the game have hit more home runs; he is the only catcher in modern history to steal more than 100 bases and hit over 100 home runs), he commands respect. But there is more. As much as any other player in baseball, he can control the tempo of a game. Indeed, he has been criticized by some opponents and members of the press for turning two-and-a-half hour games into three-hour marathons. But if a pitcher is struggling, Fisk has no qualms about slowing things down—taking just a little longer to settle into his squat or moving to the mound to exhort or lecture. When he does move, Fisk carries himself as no other player does. His manner is reminiscent of that of a thoroughbred racehorse who knows he's a winner, a strut that is part pride, part defiance. His posture when he stands on the mound is almost regal. Back straight, mask resting on his forehead like a crown, he is lord of all he surveys.

No book can paint a picture of every ball player, but Fisk seems a logical choice for our portrait of a major leaguer, a portrait of one of the watched. Why? As a catcher he is intimately involved in the action, and as a veteran he has had time to develop a healthy perspective on the proceedings. Moreover, in recent years his career has been a never-ending roller-coaster ride. He has played on a team that in 1983 won a division championship by a record number of games and then the next season experienced one of the most dramatic falls from power in the annals of the game. He has seen his tenure as a member of the White Sox threatened by trade rumors. He has seen his tenure as a catcher threatened by management's efforts to move him to a new position for his twilight years. And he has seen his entire career threatened by serious injury.

Interestingly, if Fisk had been just a little taller, his career as a baseball player might never have materialized. Growing up in tiny Charlestown, New Hampshire, he spent all his spare time "at my grandfather's barn shooting hoops," and dreamed of playing basketball for the Boston Celtics. His high school was so small that it didn't even have a football team—his third sport was soccer. As a schoolboy, he set basketball as well as baseball records, and he went to the University of New Hampshire on a basketball scholarship. (Not surprisingly, many of the game's top players also starred in other sports. Los Angeles Dodgers' outfielder Kirk Gibson was an All-American football player at Michigan State; New York Yankees' outfielder Dave Winfield earned honors playing basketball at Minnesota and was drafted by teams in the National Football League and National Basketball Association; Angels' pitcher Kirk McCaskill played minor-league hockey before turning to baseball; and most recently college football's Heisman Trophy-winner Bo Jackson, the first player selected in the 1986 NFL draft, turned down a sizable offer from the Tampa Bay Buccaneers to play baseball for the Kansas City Royals. Jackson cited the fear of serious injury on the football field as a major reason for his decision.)

Fisk's dream of wearing the Celtics' green was shattered during his freshman year at New Hampshire. "We were playing the University of Connecticut," he remembers. "Their starting guards were 6'5" and 6'6", and I was a 6'1" forward. I could jump, but it was then that I figured I better look to other sports."

Until this time, he had not taken baseball very seriously. "I never really knew anything about the game, never really cared," he says. "We only played 10 or 11 games a year in school and maybe another 10 or 11 in the summer American Legion or Babe Ruth leagues. I once tried to add up all the games I played as an amateur, and I didn't even make it to 100. That's from the ninth grade until I signed."

That signing came at age 19 in January 1967, when the Boston Red Sox picked Fisk in the first round of the winter free-agent draft. Although it's hard to imagine Fisk as anything but a catcher, it was only by chance that he ended up behind the plate. "When I was scouted, they asked me if I wanted to sign as a shortstop because I'd played shortstop in American Legion ball," he says. "Then when I did sign, the Red Sox told me they thought I could play the infield, pitch, or catch. At the time the catching situation in Boston was in doubt, and they said if I became a catcher that would be my quickest ticket to the big leagues." (Again, this is common in baseball. Remember that two All-Star Tigers, second baseman Lou Whitaker and catcher Lance Parrish, were originally third basemen but switched to hasten their trips to the majors.)

Fisk's experience as a catcher up to the day of his signing had been, to say the least, limited. "I caught in the Little League. That's where I got my nickname, Pudge. I was a little fat kid, not very tall. I caught the first three years, but the fourth year I was too fat and the equipment didn't fit me, so I played elsewhere." During his last two years in high school, he was exclusively a pitcher, and in college he caught eight out of the 13 games he played and pitched the rest.

Only a handful of ball players make it to the big leagues without playing minor-league ball. After spending 1967 in the military, Fisk was assigned to the Red Sox team in Waterloo, Iowa, for the 1968 season. In 1969, it was on to Pittsfield, Massachusetts (he did get into two games with the Red Sox at the end of that season, going hitless in five at bats). Fisk spent 1970 in Pawtucket, Rhode Island, and 1971 in Louisville before joining the Red Sox for good in September of that year. Blossoming in 1972, he batted .293, hit 22 home runs, earned a Gold Glove as the American League's top-fielding catcher, and was named Rookie of the Year. Having played so little as an amateur, how did he learn the game? "When I first came up, I spent a lot of time listening," he says. "I think most of baseball is learned asking questions and listening. Not saying 'I know' too many times. I asked a lot of questions of the old guys in the Boston organization, and then as I came up I learned a lot through the managers I played for. I also learned a lot from teammates like Reggie Smith, Carl Yastrzemski, Rico Petrocelli, and George Scott. Freddie Lynn, too. He didn't talk too much, but you could watch because he was pretty sweet the way he approached hitting. Then the guy I talked to my last four or five years in Boston was Walt Hriniak. I learned a lot about hitting from him."

Hriniak, whose philosophy and success is documented in Chapter 3, began Fisk's conversion to the Charlie Lau school of hitting. And Lau himself completed the job when he was Fisk's hitting instructor at Chicago (Fisk changed from Red to White Sox in 1981). "I'd been a down-swinger, a chopper to take advantage of Fenway," says Fisk. To take advantage of the more spacious Comiskey Park, Lau changed it so that Fisk took his top hand off the bat when he followed through instead of his bottom hand. The arc of his swing is higher, actually closer to level than before, and his arms are more extended. His front leg is almost tippy-toe prior to the pitch. Then the weight shifts.

There was no small risk in changing a stance and swing that had served Fisk well for nine full seasons and helped establish him as an offensive threat as well as a fine defensive player. "After all the success in Boston, Pudge and Charlie were both taking a chance to change his stroke," says Oakland Athletics' manager Tony LaRussa, who was Fisk's manager for over five years in Chicago.

The gamble paid off. After slumping horribly the first two months of 1983, Fisk suddenly found his swing and was one of the game's best hitters from June 1 until the end of the season. He ended up with 26 home runs and 86 runs batted in and led the Sox to a division championship. His playing time in 1984 was limited due to a serious injury, but in 1985 at age 37 he had his most productive year at the plate—107 runs batted in, and 37 home runs (33 of them while catching, a new American League record). He didn't approach those numbers in 1986 or 1987, but had an excellent year in 1988.

Fisk, like most students of the game, can detail at length the specifics of his hitting, but he prefers to speak in broader terms. "It's basically developing an approach that will work day in and day out. I've learned you have to be able to work for 162 games. On the days when you need something that's gonna work, you have to put a good pass on the ball. Because if you don't, you're gonna go 0 for 40. That's what Walt and Charlie taught me—the mechanics, physically approaching the ball properly. Then you can talk about the weight shift, the head down, the high finish, the stiff front leg and all that stuff. And when it all works together, that's when you put on your streak. With some guys like George Brett it might last two months, and with other guys, it may last five days at a time."

And where does the power come from? "It's there because you're making a good physical pass on the ball, and if you make good contact, there isn't a ball park that can hold you," Fisk explains.

While Fisk credited his 1985 home run output to good mechanics (just as his relatively poor 1986 showing was due to bad mechanics), many of his teammates believe it resulted from his intensive conditioning program, which includes midnight workouts after ballgames. The program was inaugurated shortly after a 1984 season that was disastrous both to the White Sox, who fell from first to fifth, and Fisk, who pulled an abdominal muscle on opening day and never fully recovered (he played in only 102 games, drove in only 43 runs, and saw his batting average drop 58 points from its 1983 level to .231).

"When the season ended, the Sox told me there were no miracles, that the muscle would just have to heal itself," Fisk remembers. "But I'd been waiting for that to happen and it hadn't. I'd taken more tests in one year than I'd ever taken in my whole life and all I'd found out was that I wasn't pregnant!"

He sought deliverance from Phil Claussen, a Chicago-area chiropractor who has developed conditioning programs for a number of professional athletes and has served as the Cubs' conditioning coach. "I was at a crossroads," Fisk says. "I knew if the muscle didn't heal, my career would be over. I had to do something."

That "something" was more than the catcher had ever imagined. Claussen started him on a concentrated weight-lifting program to develop body strength in general and the pulled muscle in particular. Four days a week, for as many as four hours a day, Fisk lifted free weights and did other exercises under Claussen's supervision. "One day we would work on the upper body," he says. "Then we'd take a day off. Then we'd work on the legs. Then take another day off." Fisk spent many of those "days off" at a local health club using Nautilus equipment to strengthen those areas that the free weights missed.

Fisk is not the first athlete to find the fountain of youth in a puddle of sweat. In recent years, numerous players and several ball clubs have recognized the benefits of intensive weight lifting. Most clubhouses now have weight-lifting rooms, and during the off-season, players—so well paid that they do not have to find winter employment, as ball players did a generation ago—often come to the park or a local club to work out. (A side effect of this: In the past, almost everyone used spring training to get in shape; now almost everyone reports in good condition.) Fisk, however, had never used free weights on a regular basis.

"I didn't like it, especially at the beginning, because everything I did just made the stomach muscle hurt more." Particularly painful and demanding were the leg squats. "I'd never done them before. I thought all the squatting I did behind the plate was enough," the catcher says, laughing.

The weight lifting affected Fisk's stomach in another way, too. "It made me so hungry that I ate just about anything and everything," he says. Within three months, his weight, which had dropped to 202 pounds from the end of the season was up to 230 pounds, and, he says, "heading for 260!" Claussen suggested a change in eating habits and Fisk dropped red and processed meats, salt, and fats from his diet. Salads, fish, chicken, and pasta became his new staples. By the time spring training began in 1985, his weight had leveled off at 230 pounds, and more important, the abdominal muscle had healed. A true believer in conditioning now, he has maintained the program. "Just playing baseball isn't enough to keep you in shape," he says.

This night-owl approach to training has amazed everyone in the Sox organization. "I've never seen anyone do anything like it," says Willie Thompson, the Sox's veteran clubhouse attendant, who has to wait for Fisk before he can lock up. "The man is crazy!"

When the White Sox are on the road, Fisk tries to adhere to the same schedule: "If there's a weight room in a ball park, I'll usually work out after a game. A lot of times, I won't leave until 1 A.M., and then I go back to the hotel and get room service. If the ball park doesn't have a place, I find a spot in town where I can work out during the day."

The life of a ball player, particularly a man attached to his family as Fisk is, is not as glamorous as it might appear. "People think it's glamorous because they see your picture or your name in the paper or they see you in uniform. But they have a big misconception of what it's like to be a player, or at least a conscientious player," Fisk says. "They don't see the times you get into Texas at 4 in the morning and have to play a game that same day in 100-degree weather. They say, 'Aw, you're making enough money.' It's a misconception that we're something other than human because of the money we make. We're just like everybody else. We have families, we have hurts, and we get fatigued."

As he delivers these words, Fisk is sitting in the Sox

clubhouse at the team's 1986 spring training headquarters in Sarasota, Florida. It is the dinner hour on a muggy March day, but he is still in uniform, the only player remaining at the park. His 14-year-old son Casey is at his side—the diligent father having spent a full hour after the day's exhibition game throwing batting practice to the promising young athlete. The fatigue is evident. The elder Fisk has been in the sun for over eight hours. The hurts are evident, too. Wincing as he removes his shoes and baseball stockings, Fisk examines the latest corns and contemplates an immediate harvest.

There are psychic hurts as well. After his banner 1985 season, Fisk's contract with the Sox expired and he became a free agent, able, in effect, to sell himself to the highest bidder. His family being well-established in the Chicago area, Fisk wanted to sign a three-year contract and finish his career with the White Sox. He eventually signed a two-year pact, reportedly in the neighborhood of $800,000 a year. But then the Sox tried to trade him to the Yankees for veteran designated hitter Don Baylor. The deal fell through only when Baylor exercised a trade-veto clause in his contract. At the same time, the Sox told Fisk in no uncertain terms that his days as the team's catcher were over and that come 1986 he would be playing left field. He was listed in the team's media guide and spring training programs as "outfielder."

"I was a little disappointed about how the whole off-season thing took place," Fisk says as he tosses his uniform into a laundry bin. "I didn't feel I deserved to be treated in such a small way. I'm not talking about dollar signs. I'm talking eye-to-eye, face-to-face, person-to-person—character, integrity." Particularly disturbing was the way in which the move from catcher was presented as a fait accompli. Sometimes even veterans want their hands to be held. "You need the pat on the back, the need for the team to say: 'We realize what you've done, what you are doing, is at the highest level in the game, but for the betterment of the team, this is the way we'd like to have it, and what do you think?' Instead they just issued an ultimatum: 'Do this or else.' "

But it is not only the way in which the move was handled that is bothering Fisk as the Sarasota sun begins to set. "Most people don't know anything about the catcher. All they see is his fanny as he squats behind home plate," says Duke Sims, a highly respected defensive catcher who played for 11 years and is now a minor-league manager. "But the catcher is the only player with the whole field in front of him. He's the quarterback." It is this departure from "quarterbacking" the team that is at the heart of Fisk's disenchantment. "When you're catching, you're involved with every pitch. And every pitch you're involved with could determine whether you win or lose. I've had my finger on the pulse of the game when I was catching and that meant I was mentally with it all the time. Now out in left field—nine innings, touch four balls. Catching you usually touch the ball four times before the first batter is out of the box. I might fall asleep between the ears in left and not be ready to bat," he says, pausing. "There's no recognition that I was an All-Star catcher. I *am* an All-Star catcher. I'm having a tough time dealing with that. I don't think anyone understands that I've spent 20 years perfecting my trade. I've never really considered myself an offensive player. I've concentrated on defense and how I handled the pitchers and called the game." (Fisk's observations about defense, particularly saving runs by blocking pitches, are noted in Chapter 4.)

In addition to the mental adjustment required to move from the heat of battle to its outer periphery, Fisk knew too that certain physical adjustments would be necessary—adjustments the average fan might not think of that reveal the different nature of the positions. "People don't realize I'm 38 years old. I'm not 28. I'm not 30. Most people get switched to a position that demands less conditioning and reflexes and quickness as the years go on—from left field to first base or from catcher to third base. Catching demands quickness laterally, but in left field you're talking endurance, range, speed, when you've got 2,000 games on your knees. Who knows how long they're gonna hold up?" The idea of standing around in left field until a ball was hit his way was also unappealing. "All of a sudden you have to make a play in the alley or make a play down the line and you haven't thrown for three innings other than just loosening up between innings and you haven't really run other than jogging out to your position, and now you have to bolt. But behind the plate, you've always throwing, backing up first base, always running, and if you don't feel as though you're loose you can just heat it up a little when you throw the ball back to the pitcher or run a little harder when you're backing up first base."

Less than two months after uttering these words, Fisk was back behind the plate, handling pitchers and calling games. The experiment had been a failure. Fisk had not taken well to left field, feeling as he puts it, "as strange as a whale in the desert." He committed several errors in the Sox's first 25 games, and his obvious unhappiness seemed to carry over to his hitting as well. (He was also plagued by a bad wrist.) His replacement at catcher, the highly regarded Joel Skinner (since traded to the Yankees), had difficulty throwing out base stealers and hitting the ball. And the Sox pitchers were among the least effective in baseball. The team's overall record was a disappointing 7-18.

Fisk's return to behind-the-plate duties coincided with a dramatic improvement in the Sox pitching. For those who like to look at statistics: In the games in which Fisk played left field, the staff's earned run average was a terrible 5.05; in the games in which he caught over the next 10 weeks, the ERA dropped to a respectable 3.85. (When made aware of this, Fisk, still bitter in July, said, "Well, I wish you'd tell them [management] that. The fact that I was an All-Star catcher, my catching didn't seem to have any value when they wanted to move me.")

The June renaissance of the Sox pitching staff (it would continue to have its ups and downs as the season progressed) also coincided with the arrival of a new manager, Jim Fregosi, and a new pitching coach, Dick Bosman. Watching Fisk under this new regime, a fan could not help notice that when the catcher visited pitchers on the mound his mien was meaner. Rather than giving pats on the back, he seemed to be delivering kicks to the rear end. Shortly before the All-Star break, a weary Fisk (he was suffering from a mysterious viral infection; sometimes it seemed as though he got up on the wrong side of the bed this season) acknowledged he was acting tougher: "Dunc [former pitching coach Dave Duncan] figured a pitcher's frame of mind is as important as his physical state, which is true. So you always had to be careful when you went to the mound [about upsetting that frame of mind]." And what would the fan hear if he could eavesdrop on the "new" Fisk when he visits the pitcher? "Now it's just, 'Hey, you gotta throw strikes, quality strikes. You can't fart around. You gotta go out and do it. I can't sit here and pat you on the back when you can't get anybody out." Would a pitcher rather hear that? Says Fisk, who heartily endorses the new approach, "It really doesn't make any difference what they want to hear. They [management] expect the bottom line from everybody else on the field. They ought to expect it from the pitcher. If you don't hit, you don't play. If you don't field you don't play. If you don't get anybody out, you're not supposed to play either. If you can't throw strikes, you're not supposed to pitch. That's the way it's been forever. Every pitcher knows he has to throw strikes, get ahead, stay ahead, get 'em out."

From his position behind the plate, Fisk has had an opportunity to get ahead, stay ahead, and get out some of the best hitters in the game. Whom does he most respect? "Guys like Brooks Robinson, who you thought you could knock the bat out of his hands because he looked so frail, and he'd kill you. Or Al Kaline, who you thought you could intimidate or throw the ball up and in on, and he'd take you into the bleachers. Yastrzemski and Frank Robinson. And Rod Carew and Tony Oliva, who were magicians with the bat. And now you've got Brett, Boggs, and then the strong guys in the game—Reggie Jackson, Jimmy Rice."

It is the exhilaration of the *mano-a-mano* battle with these stars that made Fisk so reluctant to move to left field. "I love the confrontation every time the good hitters come up. As a catcher, you're trying to outthink 'em, outguess 'em, outdo 'em."

Of course the pitcher has a major say in these proceedings. Fisk's favorites? "The guy I had the most fun catching was Luis Tiant." Tiant, with whom Fisk played at Boston from the time he broke in until 1978, was a seemingly ageless character with a seemingly endless variety of pitches thrown with a seemingly endless array of deliveries. Who called the pitches? "I did," says Fisk, "but he'd work on his own variation of them. I didn't call for him to look up at the sky and the center-field bleachers and stomp and snort. But I'd call a curveball and he'd deliver it any way he wanted to deliver it, up, down, in, out."

Fisk's two other favorites were former White Sox LaMarr Hoyt and Tom Seaver, both now out of baseball. When the Sox traded Hoyt, the 1983 Cy Young Award-winner, for promising shortstop Ozzie Guillen and other, lesser players after the 1984 season, Fisk was openly critical. "Being a catcher, I know the importance of a guy who can put 18 wins up and pitch 240, 250 innings," he says. (By being able to pitch that many innings a good starting pitcher can take both the pressure and the wear and tear off those in the bull pen; often, too, if a team's bull pen is not particularly effective—and the Sox would qualify here—he can simply give the manager the luxury of not having to use it.)

Fisk was also critical of the White Sox for taking so long before finally obliging Seaver's 1986 request to be traded to an East Coast team so he could finish his career closer to his Connecticut-based family. As outspoken as he has been on these occasions—making it to a ripe old age in baseball, like making it to a ripe old age in the real world, seems to give one the license to talk without worrying about what anyone thinks—Fisk more often than not appears the stereotypical tight-lipped New Englander. Having a certain amount of privacy and space are important, and he realizes he sends off vibrations to this effect. "I've had people say they hate me because of the way I walk," he says. "That it's almost a strut. And that may have been a deterrent for a lot of people in their relationship with me, because it gives the appearance that I'm unapproachable. Maybe that's my own way of creating that barrier of caution that you need to protect your ego."

If keeping a certain distance between himself and the press, fans, and even his teammates is important to Fisk ("I'm pretty solitary when we're on the road. I think it's because I'm 10 years older than most of the guys."), he is extremely close to his family. Son Casey is almost always in tow, and Fisk is a familiar figure in the crowd when his 16-year-old daughter, Carlyn, takes the basketball court for her high school. "She has the same walk I do and gets the same criticism," he says. "People come up to her and say, 'Oh, you think you're so good, just because your dad's who he is. You think you're hot stuff.'"

The time away from these loved ones takes its toll. "I've been on the road ever since I had 'em," Fisk says. "Most players don't play as long, so they get to experience a particular growth stage of their children. I haven't experienced any of them yet. You miss when they're little, when they're five, six, and they're starting to create their own personalities. By the time I get done playing, my oldest will probably be in college. So I've missed her from the time she was born to the time she was out of the house. Which really tugs. It really does. I don't think I can ever, ever forgive the game for that. You know the saying, 'Besebol been bery bery good to me,' (from the old "Saturday Night Live"). Well, it has. It's allowed us to do a lot of things that most families don't get to do. But the one thing it hasn't allowed us is being together."

When he isn't instructing his own kids in sports—as a father he admits to being frustrated by most of the instruction they receive—Fisk can be found in the dirt at his home outside Chicago—but not in his catcher's squat. "During the last couple of years I've been establishing a garden," he explains. "And I raise orchids. It's very relaxing. I can be out there for hours and get lost, and all of a sudden I'm supposed to go to the ball park."

Whether he retires to this garden remains to be seen. Because they are so involved in the strategy of the game, catchers are particularly well suited to make the transition from the playing field to coaching, managing, or broadcasting. Says Fisk: "Staying in the game is a possibility. I've learned a lot over the years. But whether I really know what I learned probably won't be apparent until I stop playing and then reflect on it, and then try to clue kids in on what it takes to play the game."

When he does eventually retire, the image of Carlton Fisk that will remain in most fans' minds is one of the most indelible baseball moments of the last quarter-century. Fisk stands at home plate in Fenway Park having just slammed a ball that, if it stays in fair territory, will be a home run. Not just any home run, it will win the sixth game of the 1975 World Series for the Red Sox. The usually undemonstrative hitter is animated now, coaxing, now, *directing* the ball with his entire body to land fair. When it becomes clear the ball has obeyed, he jumps up and down, and only after what seems like forever starts the happy journey around the bases. Over a decade later, Fisk characterizes the moment as "dreamlike, almost like it didn't happen to me."

Is this the image he would most like to leave behind?

Fisk: "It's really strange because I think people view you as so important while you're playing and then when you're done they don't view you as important, which is really sad because that means they're basically fronting you. I've seen guys play the game and be recognized as the best and two years after they're done all people say is, 'Oh, yeah, I remember he played.' I just hope that throughout the course of my career, I showed them that I came to play hard every day and I tried to do the best job I could and was a pretty dang good ball player."

What player could ask for anything more? And what fan would be so blind as to disagree?

INDEX

INDEX

Acker, Jim, 169
Alexander, Doyle, 158-159, 169
Allen, Neil, 158, 160-162, 164
Allen, Richie, 38
Anderson, Sparky, 19, 20, 25-27, 72, 162-163, 168
  five-man rotation system used by, 39-40
Andujar, Joaquin, 125-126, 168
Announcers, wrong calls by, 45-46
Armas, Tony, 59, 64, 80
The Art of Pitching, 31, 39
Artificial turf vs. natural grass, 85-86
Astroturf, 94

Backman, Wally, 3, 8
Baines, Harold, 121, 122, 159-160, 165, 167, 172-173
Balboni, Steve, 118, 121, 122, 130, 132, 133
Ballparks
  dimensions of, 33
  importance of, 55
  see also names of specific parks
Bannister, Floyd, 117, 161, 162
Barfield, Jesse, 19, 159, 161

Barrett, Marty, 62-63, 175
Base stealing, 93-109
  astroturf and, 94
  batting behind, 101-102
  invention of, 93-94
Battery, 28
Batting cage, 6
Batting practice, 7, 11-12
Batting. *See* Hitting
Baylor, Don, 63, 152, 176, 177
  mental adjustment made by, 187-188
Beanball incidents, 17-18
Beattie, Jim, 174
Bell, George, 159, 161, 164
Berra, Dale, 91
Bettencourt, Dave, 30, 31
Biancalana, Buddy, 119-120, 121, 122, 127-128, 130, 133
Blaylock, Gary, 118, 119
Boggs, Wade, *xvi*, 19, 56, 60-61, 190
Bombers: *see* New York Yankees
Bonilla, Bobby, 163, 167, 169
Bonilla, Juan, 175
Bosman, Dick, 189-190
Boston, Daryl, 159
Boston Red Sox, 20-21, 51-68
  hitting figures (1985), 56
Bouton, Jim, *xii*
BP: *see* Batting practice

Breaking pitch: *see*
  Curveball
Bremigan, Nick, 137
Brett, George, *xvi*, 34, 55,
  56, 73-74, 78, 82, 113,
  115, 117, 119, 120, 121,
  125, 129, 131, 132, 141,
  142, 144, 149, 184, 190
Brinkman, Ed, 72, 73, 86
Brock, Lou, 94
Buckner, Bill, 51, 52, 63-64,
  152, 175

Cangelosi, John, 70, 159-160,
  164, 167, 169
Capparelli, Frank, 1
"Captain Hook": *see*
  Anderson, Sparky
Carew, Rod, 190
Carlisle, Belinda, 174
Carlton, Steve, 105
Carter, Gary, 7-8, 9, 12, 17,
  106, 108, 142
Catchers
  described, 91
  on-field communication by,
    139
  weight distribution of, 90
Cedeno, Cesar, 128, 131
Cey, Ron, 10
Change-up pitch, 49
Chicago Tribune, 5
Chicago White Sox, 155-169
  1982 and 1983 seasons, 72
  Toronto Blue Jays vs.
    (5/21/86), 158-169
Clark, Jack, 42, 132
Claussen, Phil, 185-186
Clemens, Roger, 21-22, 174,
  176
Clubhouse, 7-9
Cobb, Ty, 94
Coleman, Vince, *xvi*, 80, 93,
  94, 97, 102, 105, 106

Comiskey Park, *xii*, 111
  Harrelson's shenanigans
    at, 156
  hitting technique for, 183
  observation of game from
    dugout, 173-177
Commerce Comet: *see* Mantle,
  Mickey
Communication, on-field: *see*
  On-field communication
Computer printouts, 117
  pre-game preparation and,
    2-3
Concepcion, Onix, 122, 132,
  133
Cooper, Cecil, 85, 117
Cowley, Joe, 69-70
Cox, Danny, 123, 129
Craig, Roger
  split-finger fastball, 46-
    47
Cruz, Julio, 81-82, 121, 173
Curveball, 33, 47-49

Darling, Ron, 7, 15, 18
  pre-game routine, 9-10,
    16-17
Davis, Jody, 101, 107-109,
  142
Dayley, Ken, 131-132
Defense, 71-92
  blocking pitches, 90
  catcher's weight
    distribution, 90
  see also Fielding
Dempsey, Rick, 142, 152, 176
Denkinger, Don, 114
Dernier, Bobby, 95, 96, 102
Detroit Tigers, 19-21
Dixon, Ken, 152-153, 174-177
Dotson, Rich, 165
Drabowsky, Moe, 146, 157
Drug scandals, 8
Drysdale, Don, 39

Duncan, Dave, 190
Dunston, Shawn, 41
Duvalier, "Baby Doc," 53

Easler, Mike, 59-60, 62, 63
Eckersley, Dennis, 2
Eichhorn, Mark, 169
Einhorn, Eddie, 162
Elias Sports Bureau, 117
Evans, Dwight, 41, 52, 64, 79-80, 84-85, 86, 152-153, 176, 177
Exercise programs, 9, 185-186

Fans
    hitters, suggestions for watching, 67-68
    pitchers, guidelines for watching, 44-45
    pre-game preparation, 170
    taunting by, 42-43
    viewing techniques, 169-177
Farr, 121
Fastball, 21-22
    rising, 46
    split-finger, 46-47
Fenway Park, 193
    "dungeon" in, 51, 54
    Green Monster, 55
    Harrelson at, 156
    hitting technique for, 183
    right field, 84
Fernandez, Sid, 9
Fernandez, Tony, 162
Ferraro, 119
Fielding
    covering first, 88
    Gold Glove award for, 72-73
    pitchers' ability at, 87
    practice, 16
    pre-game preparation, 13
    reading catcher's signs, 77-78
    sacrifice bunt, 88-89
    see also Defense
Film used to analyze players' strengths and weaknesses, 56
Finley, Charles O., 156
Fireovid, Steve, 175
Fisk, Carlton, 56, 90-92, 101-102, 112, 120, 121, 160, 164, 165, 180-193
Fisk, Carlyn, 192
Fisk, Casey, 192
Ford, Whitey, 161, 166
Forkball, 38, 46
Foster, George, 7, 8, 16
Fraternization, pre-game, 14
Frazier, George, 3
Fregosi, Jim, 157, 189-190
"The Freshest Man on Earth." See Latham, Artie
Frey, Jim, 95, 102, 113
Fungoes, 13

Garcia, Damaso, 60, 158, 162, 165
Garland, Steve, 3, 4, 6, 9, 16
Gedman, Rich, 51, 52, 61-62, 64-66, 85
"The Georgia Peach." See Cobb, Ty
Gibson, Bob, 33
Gibson, Kirk, 143-144, 181
Gold Glove award, 72-73
Gooden, Dwight, 6, 15, 22
    rising fastball, 46
Grass, natural vs. artificial turf, 85-86
Grich, Bobby, 160
Grubb, John, 145
Guerrero, Pedro, 83
Guidry, Ron, 82, 86-89, 140-141, 147

covering first, 88
sacrifice bunt, 88-89
Guillen, Ozzie, 82, 91, 117, 159, 167, 173, 191
Gullickson, Bill, 103, 104

Hairston, Jerry, 112, 169
Haiti, baseballs manufactured in, 53
Hansen, Ron, 86
Harper, Brian, 131
Harrassment by fans, 42-43
Harrelson, Bud, 5, 8, 9, 11, 12, 170
  pre-game weather check, 13-14
Harrelson, Ken "Hawk," 21, 55
  houseboy (Wendell), 156-157
  viewing Toronto Blue Jays vs. Chicago White Sox game of 5/21/86, 155-169
Hassey, Ron, 143-144
Hearn, Ed, 17
Hemond, Roland, 56
Henderson, Dave, 175
Henderson, Ricky, 82, 93, 101
  base stealing by, 94, 95-96
Hernandez, Keith, 6, 7, 8, 9, 158
Hernandez, Willie, 40
Herr, Tommy, 81
Herzog, Whitey, 102, 104-105, 125, 132, 134, 168
Higgins, George V., 177
Higuera, Ted, xvi
Hitting, 47-70
  batting cage, 6
  batting practice, 7, 11-12
  behind a base stealer, 101-102
  home runs, 66

Lau-Hriniak theory: see Hriniak, Walt; Lau, Charlie
  mental attitude, 25
  setting up pitchers, 38
  suggestions for watching, 67-68
  sweet spot, 66-67
  thinking part of, 59
  videotape used to study, 62
Home runs, 66
Hoscheit, Vern, 7, 10-11, 14, 145-146
  background, 2
  batting practice described by, 12
  pre-game routine, 2-3
Houk, Ralph, 12, 116
Howser, Dick, 111-135, 137, 168
  art of managing discussed by, 114-116
  computer printouts used by, 117
  Elias Sports Bureau reports used by, 117
  illness of, 134-135
  lineup by, 115-116
  scouting reports used by, 116
Hoyt, LaMarr, 191
Hriniak, Walt, 14, 32, 51-53, 54-55, 57-59, 60-61, 64-67, 183
Hunter, Catfish, 17

Injuries, 4, 162-163
  as cause of last-minute lineup changes, 118
  chiropractor used to help, 185-186
Iorg, Dane, 133

Jackson, Bo, 181
Jackson, Reggie, 34-35, 77-78, 81-82, 190
  observation of players by, 179
  on-field communication, 139, 141, 142
  pre-game preparation, 172-173
  varying roles, 144-145
Jefferson, Jesse, 97-98
John, Tommy, 28-29, 37
Johnson, Cliff, 161
Johnson, Davey, 2, 4, 5, 9, 14, 15, 16, 18
Johnson, Howard, 8
Jones, Lynn, 120

Kaline, Al, 155, 167-168, 171, 190
Kansas City Royals, 111-135
  World Series (1985), 122-134
Keyser, Ken, 142
Kibler, John, 16, 17, 139-140, 141, 143
  pre-game preparation, 14
King, Eric, 21
Kittle, Ron, 163-164, 165, 169
Knight, Ray, 6-7, 8, 12, 18
Knuckleball, 46
Kuhn, Bowie, 156

Landrum, Tito, 131
LaPoint, Dave, 20, 21, 25, 27
LaRussa, Tony, 101-102, 157, 162, 169, 183
Lasorda, Tommy, 113, 138, 141, 146
Latham, Arlie, 93-94
Lau, Charlie, 56-57, 58, 64-67, 183
Law, Rudy, 102, 159

Lee, Bill, 79
Leibrandt, Charlie, 112, 113-114, 120-127, 130-131, 133
Leyland, Jim, 76-77, 147
Lineup card, 10-11
Lopes, Davey, 10, 18
Lynn, Freddie, 183

Maas, Duke, xiii
Malkin, John, 17
Manager, 111-135
  importance of, 114-115
Mantle, Mickey, xi et seq.
Maris, Roger, 156
Marshall, Mike, 174
Martin, Billy, 113, 128, 157
Matthews, Gary, 3, 41
Mattingly, Don, 19, 45, 56, 68-70, 73, 82, 87, 142
  preparation by, 75-76
Mauch, Gene, xvi, 105
Mays, Willie, 151
Mazeroski, Bill, 86
McCaskill, Kirk, 181
McDowell, Roger, 105, 142
McGee, Willie, 53, 73, 75, 80, 83, 102, 131
McGregor, Scott, 37
McKeon, Joel, 70
McMurtry, Craig, 105
McRae, Hal, 118, 119, 121, 133, 143, 144
Meacham, Bobby, 91
Miller, Ray, 96, 102-103
Miller, Stu, 163
Mitchell, Kevin, 3, 4
Mitchelson, Marvin, 158
Moreland, Keith, 3
Morgan, Joe, 95, 96, 97, 98, 105-106, 166
Morris, Jack, 20-21, 25, 29, 34-35
  pitching demeanor, 26-27

Moseby, Lloyd, 158, 159, 163, 165-167
Mota, Manny, 145
Motley, Darryl, 117, 132
Muffett, Billy, 19, 21, 23, 28, 29-30, 31-32, 33, 36-37, 147
Mulliniks, Rance, 158, 166, 167
Munson, Thurman, 142-143
Murphy, Dale, 73
Murray, Eddie, 19-20, 100, 175

National League
  batting practice rules, 7
Nelson, Dave, 97-98, 100-101, 103, 104
Nelson, Gene, 70
Nettles, Graig, 85
New York Mets
  pre-game preparation, 1-18
New York Yankees, *xi et seq.*
  typical day, 68-70
Nichols, Reid, 69, 121
Niekro, Joe, 79
Niemann, Randy, 145
Nossek, Joe, 149-150

Oates, Johnny, 96, 107-108
Observing the players,
  importance of, 172-173, 179-193
Ojeda, Bob, 5, 15
Oliva, Tony, 85, 190
On-field communication, 137-153
  etiquette of, 139
  friendly banter, 142
  pump sign system, 152
  stealing signs, 149-153
Orta, Jorge, 118, 132

Pagliarulo, 151

Palermo, Steve, 158-159, 161
Parrish, Lance, 29, 30, 31, 32, 86, 89, 90, 182
  catchers described by, 91
Patterson, Floyd, *xii*
Pena, Tony, 142
Pendleton, Terry, 131
Personality, effect of, 172-173
Pesky, Johnny, 56
Petrocelli, Rico, 183
Petry, Dan, 20, 21, 23, 24, 28, 34, 72
Phelps, Ken, 174-175
Piniella, Lou, 147-148
"Pitch of the 80s," 46
Pitchers
  American League, 35
  arms, trauma to, 35-38
  bull pen, in the, 145-146
  demeanor of, 26-27
  fielding ability of, 87
  five-man rotation, 15, 39-40
  guidelines for watching, 44-45
  left-handed, 99-101
  legs, strength of, 36-37
  mental attitude needed by, 24-26
  pre-game preparation, 10, 15
  relief, 16, 145-146
  relief specialist, 40-45
  rhythm, 100
  right-handed, 98-99
  starting, 15, 27
  watching, suggestions for, 98-100
Pitching
  breaking pitches, 47-49
  change-up, 49
  coach, 146-147
  curveball, 33, 47-49

direction of pitch, 22-23
fastball, 21-22
forkball, 38, 46
"framing" pitches, 30
game plan, 28
importance of, 19-49
knuckleball, 46
mounds, 32, 33
rhythm of, 32-33
rising fastball, 46
screwball, 48
setting up hitters, 38
sinker, 46
slider, 47-49
speed of throw, 35-36, 41-42
split-finger fastball, 46-47
split-fingered sinker-screwball, 38
stopper, 40-44
strikeouts vs. outs, 38
trouble spots, 30-34
types of, 21-25
videotape used to pinpoint problems, 31
wrong calls by announcers, 45-46
Porter, Darrell, 128, 131
Pre-game preparation, 1-18
for viewers, 170

Quick, Jim, 125
Quirk, Jamie, 133
Quisenberry, Dan, 111-112, 113, 114, 119, 121, 122, 123, 130, 131, 133

Raines, Tim, 94, 97, 101, 105, 106
Randolph, Willie, 82
Reardon, Jeff, 14, 145
harrassment by fans, 42-43
rising fastball, 46

stopper, background as a, 40-44
Reese, Pee Wee, 71
Reinsdorf, Jerry, 56
Relaxation, pre-game, 8
Reynolds, Harold, 174, 175
Rice, Jim, 60, 63, 66, 80, 175-176, 190
Riley, George, 41
Robinson, Bill, 5, 6-7, 13, 16, 17, 18
batting practice, 11-12
Robinson, Brooks, 71, 190
Robinson, Frank, 190
Rodgers, Bob, 41
Rodriguez, Aurelio, 89
Romero, Ed, 175, 177
Rookie of the Year (1985), 159
Rose, Pete, 4
Ruth, George Herman ("Babe"), 71
Ryan, Nolan, 22, 33

Saberhagen, Bret, 123, 133
Salazar, Luis, 111-112, 121
Sandberg, Ryne, 41, 102, 106
Santana, Rafael
pre-game preparation, 13
"Saturday Night Live," 192
Schmidt, Dave, 162, 163, 164-165, 167, 168-169
Schofield, Dick, 173
Schuerholz, John, 114-115
Scioscia, Mike, 91, 139, 140, 142, 146
Scoreboard, 172
Scoring the game, 171
Scott, George, 183
Scouting reports, 116
pre-game preparation, 3
Screwball, 48
Seattle Mariners, 173-177

Seaver, Tom, 30-31, 39, 119, 152, 161, 162, 173, 191
    astroturf's effect on the game, 94
    tactics to avoid base stealing, 103
Shea Stadium batting cage, 6
Sheridan, Pat, 127, 130, 132
Sikes, Bob, 3, 4, 6, 16
Sims, Duke, 172, 188
Sinker, 46
Sinker-screwball, split-fingered, 38
Sisk, Doug, 15
Skinner, Joel, 82, 189
Slider, 47-49
Smith, Lonnie, 119, 120, 122, 124, 125, 128, 129
Smith, Ozzie, xvi, 71, 74, 77-79, 80, 81, 85, 129, 131
Smith, Reggie, 183
The Spaulding Guide, 93
Sporting News poll, 113
Sports equipment salesmen, 8
Sports, transfer of baseball skills to other, 181-182
St. Louis Cardinals
    1985 World Series, 122-134
Steinbrenner, George, 112
Stengel, Casey, xi
Stone, Steve, 23-24, 27-28, 32-33, 39, 45
Stottlemyre, Mel, 4-5, 6, 10, 11, 14, 15, 16, 17, 146-147
    pre-game preparation, 170-171
Strawberry, Darryl, 7, 8, 12, 16
Sullivan, Haywood, 83, 169
Sundberg, Jim, 115, 127, 130, 133
Sutton, Don, 158

Tanana, Frank, 20, 143
    background, 36-38
Tartabull, Danny, 174
Team manager: see Manager
"The Terminator": see Reardon, Jeff
Terrell, Jerry, 116-117
Terrell, Walt, 20, 21, 29, 31, 33-34, 35, 138
    sinker, 46
Thompson, Willie, 186
Tiant, Luis, 79, 191
Tolleson, Wayne, 82, 164
Toronto Blue Jays, 155-169
    vs. Chicago White Sox (5/21/86), 158-169
Training room, 7-9
Trammell, Alan, xvii, 81
Tudor, John, 30, 71-72, 123
Turley, Bob, xiii

Umpires
    on-field communication, 138-141
    pre-game preparation, 14, 16
Upshaw, Willie, 160, 161, 164

Valenzuela, Fernando, 105
Videotape
    hitters studied on, 62
    instructional use of, 6
    leading off studied on, 104
    pitching problems, used to pinpoint, 31
Viewers: see Fans
Viewing techniques, 169-177
Vukovich, John, 17

Walker, Greg, 160, 165, 167
Wallach, Tim, 77, 78, 86
Waner, Paul, 56
Washington, Claudell, 69

Watching the game, 155-177
Weather, pre-game check of, 13
Weight lifting, 185-186
Wendell, 156-157
Westrum, Wes, 151
Weyer, Lee, 138
Whitaker, Lou, *xvi*, 73, 74, 78, 81, 89, 182
White, Frank, 24, 74, 111-112, 121, 126-127, 144
Whitt, Ernie, 161-162
Williams, Ted, 55, 60, 64, 167
    batting theories, 57-59
    hitters, how to watch, 67-68
    hitting described by, 52, 53
Wills, Maury, 166
Wilson, Willie, 82, 83, 118, 120, 124, 129, 131-132

Winfield, Dave, 11, 73, 77, 79, 82, 83-84, 86, 92, 141, 171, 181
World Series (1975), 193
World Series (1985), 168
    game 6, 122-134
Worrell, Todd, 132, 133
Wrigley Field
    ground rules, 18
    pre-game routine, 1-18
    weather, 13
    workout room, 9

Yankee Stadium, *xii et seq.*
Yastrzemski, Carl, 55, 183, 190
Yeager, Steve, 142

Zimmer, Don, 143, 147-148, 150-151